CHRIST THE KING OF GLORY

Also by Dom Anscar Vonier

Published by Assumption Press

The Human Soul and its Relations with Other Spirits

The Personality of Christ

A Key to the Doctrine of the Eucharist

The Christian Mind

The Divine Motherhood

The Life of the World to Come

The Art of Christ: Retreat Conferences

The Angels

Death and Judgement

The New and Eternal Covenant

Christianus

The Victory of Christ

The Spirit and the Bride

The People of God

Sketches and Studies in Theology

CHRISTOLOGICAL TRILOGY II

CHRIST THE KING OF GLORY

Tu Rex Gloriae Christe

DOM ANSCAR VONIER

2013

✠ Nihil Obstat.
Edward J. Mahony, S.T.D.,
Censor Deputatus.

✠ Imprimatur.
Joseph Butt,
Vicarius Generalis.

Westminster
February 22, 1932

The *Nihil Obstat* and *Imprimatur* are official declarations
that a book or pamphlet is free of doctrinal or moral error.
No implication is contained therein that those who have
granted the *Nihil Obstat* and the *Imprimatur* agree
with the content, opinions or statements expressed.

This book was originally published in 1932
by Burns, Oates, and Washbourne.

Cover image: *The Resurrection,* detail from the Isenheim Altarpiece,
Matthias Grünewald, 1512-16

CONTENTS

FOREWORD

T HE FOLLOWING PAGES WERE ORIGINALLY THEOLOGICAL lectures delivered by myself to the younger members of the Abbey. They are a free rendering, but I think a very exact one, of all the essential points of the teaching of St. Thomas Aquinas concerning the mystery of the Incarnation. On a second perusal of the lectures the impression gained ground in my mind that a wider public might be helped by them. On the whole very few people have the leisure or the intellectual equip¬ment to do justice to the text of St. Thomas, though they are quite capable otherwise of following a theological exposition, even of the more exacting kind. For such readers these pages are sent forth. From the first chapter to the last they contain nothing but precise and even technical theological thought. If the reader is fortunate enough to be able to read the Summa in the text he will have no difficulty in discovering in the articles of St. Thomas all that is said here.

One more word in order to justify my venture. It is not an enviable state to have a reputation for writing difficult books; but it is with a very good intention that I undertake this unpopular task. The science of Christ is the greatest of all sciences, so we cannot expect its study to be as easy as the perusal of a storybook. It requires an effort of the mind to understand what is meant by Hypostatic Union and all the marvellous consequences that flow from it. This book is really a contribution towards the fuller apprehension of the traditional faith that enables us to say that God was born for us, that God died for us, and that Mary is truly the Mother of God.

Anscar Vonier, O.S.B.
Abbot of Buckfast
Buckfast Abbey,
Feast of the Immaculate Conception, 1931.

1

THE CONGRUITY OF THE INCARNATION

THE INCARNATION IS A WORK OF GOD'S OMNIPOTENT power. The early Fathers and Doctors of the Church agree in calling it his greatest work, but it conforms to the lines of those other divine activities which constitute the Christian theology of creation, as opposed to all other theories which may be classed under the name of pantheism.

The fundamental principle of Christian theology is to be found in the admission of God's supreme goodness, and of the power and will of that goodness to communicate itself outside itself. This communication is not made through a bestowal of God's own nature, or of a portion of that nature, but through God's power as efficient Cause to bring into being things which are more and more perfect and which increasingly resemble the divine goodness. This participation by the creature in God's goodness must be understood in the terms of a resemblance to God, of a similarity between the finite creature and the infinite Creator, which becomes more and more accentuated. It is thus that God is said to communicate himself *ad extra*, "outwardly"; the Incarnation is no departure from that universal concept of Christian theology with regard to the nature of being and with regard to the relation between the Creator and the creature.

The endless possibilities of God's power to communicate his goodness in the sense thus described have always been admitted by those who worship God in spirit and in truth. Christian theology, from its very genius, is ready to accept any marvel, however immeasurable, in the order of nature. The discoveries of science in the realm of physical reality are but a confirmation of the Christian faith in a Creator of infinite goodness. In the supernatural sphere Christian theology is ready for greater marvels still. Not only do we believe in a spirit world much more immense and much more extensive than the physical universe—and this is still within the natural order of things—but we hold that, through grace, God communicates himself more and more abundantly, bringing about resemblances with himself in those who constitute the family of the children of God, and who are so not only in name but in reality, because their similarity with God is so close. There remains, however, a third possibility, one that is greater than God's communication of himself either through his marvellous power of creation or through supernatural grace. The third possibility is this: that God should bestow his own personal being on an individual of a finite nature, yet in such a mode that the incommunicable nature of God should not become in any way diminished through that participation. We do not pretend that it would have been within the power of a finite mind, much less of a human mind, to think out such a possibility; but after it has been shown to us by revelation we are at least able to see how this mode of divine communication does not differ essentially from other ways of divine communication, but is simply a more excellent way in which God bestows himself.

So Incarnation is defined as "the communication of the divine personal Being on a created nature through the goodness of God." It is essentially a bestowal, a gift, an act of God *ad extra*, of the same order as the creative act through which he produced the world, visible and invisible, as an image of himself. How in this mode of communication there is no sort of pantheism will be explained later. Very guardedly, Catholic theology says that this third and supreme way for God to communicate himself is by bestowing his personal Being on a creature. We do not say that God bestows his own nature on a creature. In this lies the whole difference between Incarnation and so-called emanation; emanation would mean the gift of God's own nature, a concept entirely repugnant to Christian theology. But this we must leave to a later chapter; here we only would make it clear that the Incarnation is one of God's works, and, like all his works *ad extra*, it is a communication of divine goodness through God's omnipotent power.

So we may say at once that the Incarnation as it is taught by the Church is in most complete accord with all the traditional Christian philosophy of being. It is in no way contrary to that kind of ontology which has always been accepted by Christian thought. The immutable does not change into the mutable, the infinite does not change into the finite; the greater thing is not sacrificed to the smaller, nor does the unlimited grow limited. Conceiving, as we do, the Incarnation to be a work of God's infinite power, we do not restrict the Divinity when we say that he became Man, because that very thing—his becoming Man—in no way detracts from the divine power, any more than the creation of one world takes away from him or diminishes in him the might of making other worlds without end. Most of the objections against the Incarnation, which men at all times have brought forward, and which the Doctors of the Church have made it their business to refute, come from this fundamental misconception, that they viewed the Incarnation as a modification of God's Being, whereas it is a communication of God's Being without any modification of it. All the immutations are on the side of the created nature which God calls into a participation in his personal Being. The degree of that privileged nature in the scale of beings matters little, as all the differentiations of created nature come from God. Therefore it cannot be said that a nature is fundamentally unworthy of such a preference, since God himself willed the relative position of every creature in the scheme of the universe. Moreover, this admission of a finite nature into participation with the divine personal Being is infinitely above the deserts of all creatures put together, and so it matters little on which of his creatures God bestows participation in his personal Being. Thus it may be said that, from the ontological point of view, there exists no kind of incongruity in the Christian concept of the Incarnation.

All Christian Doctors, following in this the Scriptures themselves, have abounded in bringing forth reasons which establish the supreme appropriateness of the Incarnation from the ethical or spiritual point of view. It is truly the main theme of all Christian preaching. Of course, it is evident that a work like the Incarnation, when once we admit its ontological validity and possibility, must have in its favor every conceivable and imaginable ethical or spiritual usefulness. The only point concerning which there could be a doubt and round which controversies have existed is whether the Incarnation was a necessary and unavoidable dispensation for the salvation of mankind, so that man could not have been saved if God had not become incarnate. The Catholic teachers are unanimous in rejecting any such obligation for God. They say that it would have been within the divine power to bring about the Redemption in entirely different ways, and these without number. There is, however, one very important matter which has received much attention from the post-Tridentine Fathers and to which the older Doctors like St. Thomas already alluded, though without making of this question the pivot of the doctrine of the purposes of the Incarnation, as did later theologians. Human sin is said to be an offence against God's majesty and has therefore a kind of infinity of injustice against God. Now, it is possible that God may forgive all sin, and in doing so he would not renounce the claims of his justice, for, as St. Thomas says:

> God has no superior and he himself is the supreme and common good of the whole universe; and therefore if he remits sin which has the nature of guilt because it is committed against himself, he does no injustice to anyone (*Summa*, III q. 76, a. 2, ad 3).

But in the hypothesis that God wants the human race to give full satisfaction for the sin committed by man, it would seem that in such a supposition it would be necessary to have a human nature of infinite dignity in order to made adequate amends for sin.

In this very restricted sense only would Catholic theologians speak of the Incarnation as being in any way necessary; because there is a real impossibility of attaining a certain end without the definite means of the Incarnation; the end is full satisfaction for sin given to God by human nature: this end could not be achieved unless human nature be divine.

St. Thomas, after enumerating all the immense advantages which come to the human race through the Incarnation, says very wisely, "But there are many other advantages which come from the Incarnation which are above the ken of the human mind" (III, q. 1 a. 2).

Perhaps the most complete form in which the purpose of the Incarnation could be expressed is the one made use of by St. Paul in his first Epistle to the Corinthians:

> For by a man came death: and by a man the resurrection of the dead. And as in Adam all die, so also in Christ shall all be made alive (1 Cor 15:21-22).

The central idea of St. Paul is evidently that Christ is the supernatural head of mankind, as Adam was the natural head. As the supernatural head of fallen humanity the God-Man, Christ, is supremely fitted to carry out the work of raising up the race. Only an infinite Person could have a redeeming influence on the souls of all possible men. The purposes for which Christ is said to have come are nowhere enumerated in a logical order; indeed, they could not well be classified. The New Testament is full of passages of supreme eloquence each of which states the Incarnation in terms of universal efficacy. Whether Christ be considered as atoning for sin, as reconciling man with God, as destroying the power of Satan, as putting an end to death, as giving life, as redeeming man, as teaching the way of happiness, as leading us into all truth, the inspired writer never makes any restrictions or reservations. In all these capacities and offices Christ is said to be not only final but absolutely universal.

Though the work of the Incarnation has about it this pervading character of infinitude, still Catholic theology has never failed to remember that, like all the works of God *ad extra*, it is a contingent work; therefore the putting forth of that work would be conditioned by such contingent happenings as the fall of man. In other words, Catholic theology finds no lack of proportion in this, that so great a mystery as the Incarnation should depend on man's sin, or rather, should be essentially a remedy of sin, not an absolute gift. Therefore the gravest theologians, and among them St. Thomas, say that if man had not sinned the Incarnation would not have taken place. And the Doctors of the Church find nothing disproportionate in the taking of manhood by God in order to heal the sin of man. There have been, of course, minds which have found it difficult to profess unreservedly that the Incarnation was only a remedy for sin. The Incarnation, they say, was decreed independently of sin, as the supreme manifestation of God's infinite power: sin came after, and the Incarnation received the secondary purpose, that of being the remedy of sin. St. Thomas does not absolutely reject such idealism. However, he wants it to be understood that it is perfectly wise to admit an Incarnation which would be directly and primarily the remedy of sin.

Some writers see in the Incarnation the occasion for God to show forth infinitude of power; but St. Thomas remarks very appropriately that such infinitude is shown forth in the production of every created thing.

From what precedes it is easy to understand that the one evil which Christ came to cure is the universal evil of mankind—original sin, with all its consequences. For this reason the Scriptures as well as Catholic tradition are so insistent on the circumstance that Christ took upon himself all the burdens which are the inheritance of fallen man and, chief amongst them, the burden of death. A Christ who did not share human conditions to the full or who in his life and death had experiences which were not human at all would not be the Christ of Catholic theology:

> Wherefore, it behooved him in all things to be made like unto
> his brethren, that he might become a merciful and faithful high

priest before God, that he might be a propitiation for the sins of his people. For in that wherein he himself hath suffered and been tempted he is able to succor them also that are tempted (Heb 2:17-18).

This universality of influence on the part of the God Incarnate over the human race is also the idea to which we must recur should we ask ourselves the question why the Incarnation took place when it did. We cannot, of course, produce any reason why the Son of God should have been born of Mary in the days of Augustus, but at least satisfaction is granted to our minds in the certainty that a head of infinite power would react on the human race in all directions, surmounting all obstacles, at whatever period of the world's history he might choose to appear.

2

ON THE KIND OF UNION
BETWEEN GOD AND MAN
IN THE INCARNATION

IT IS ADMITTED ON ALL HANDS THAT THE INCARNATION implies union between God and man. We ask now what is the special kind of union which makes of the Incarnation an entirely new mystery in the supernatural order.

We must at once discard the idea of a union which would be merely moral, such as is the bond of friendship, the bond of allegiance or the bond of obedience. Such a linking up between God and man, though of supreme ethical importance, would by no means do justice to the Incarnation. Nor would that higher union which consists in grace and charity be sufficient to explain the Incarnation; for this kind of union is common to all the Saints of God and would not differentiate the Incarnation from ordinary sanctity, even if grace and charity were present in the highest degree imaginable; for this would only make a difference of degree, not a difference of kind. The Incarnation unites man with God, not only in a higher degree, but in a different way from ordinary sanctity, otherwise it could not be "the mystery, which had been hidden from ages and generations" (Col 1:26).

In order to make clear this entirely new mode of union between God and man, Catholic theology puts forward two possible modes of union between two distinct beings, modes which are absolutely real and which are not contained in those already described. One of these two new modes is called by theologians "union in nature," the other is called "union in person"—Unio in natura, unio in persona. We must understand that these two ways of being united are found in creatures and are known by observation; and we make use of these two very clear concepts concerning union in order to explain the divine mystery. As in all other portions of Catholic theology, we take for granted that the human concepts arrived at by experience are valid enough to be applied analogically to the divine order of things; so that we are truly speaking sense when we express the mysteries of God in the ideas arrived at through human perception.

The first and most direct way for two things to become one, or to be united, is this: that they are made one through a change. Either the separate entities lose their respective properties, to become through their union a new thing altogether, or the stronger nature absorbs and assimilates the weaker. Change in both these cases is of the very essence of the union. In these very general terms theologians describe what they call unio in natura; a conversion of being from one definite kind into another definite kind is implied in this formula. This, the most universal mode by which physical realities are brought together, is not admissible in the doctrine of the Incarnation. It goes too far. It would mean, in the most favorable interpretation, a complete absorption by the Godhead of the manhood, as food is assimilated by a living organism. Or, in the crudest interpretation, a change in the eternal Godhead itself, as entering into composition with a created nature, to make one by the mutual conversion of the two. This, of course, is unthinkable, it being incompatible with the supremest of God's qualities, that of absolute immutability of nature.

We come, therefore, to the second mode of union observable in creation: unio in persona. It is of a more subtle kind, which hardly strikes the imagination, but which is the constant theme of philosophers. Take a complete being, such as man. In that being we observe a stable element, a permanent substance, so to speak, which is the cause that such a one is the same person from birth to death. At the same time there are in such a being endless phenomena, such as emotion and thought; there are, moreover, realities which do not belong to the very essence of that man. Since they change so considerably they are termed "accidents" in philosophic phraseology. Thus the same human being varies immensely in its quantitive aspect—to speak of one "accident" only. All the external acts of that man are phenomena which manifest themselves in endless varieties of time and quantity. But the prevailing fact is this: that all such things, which are so rightly called accidental, are still intimately united with that being, with that subject; they are radically his, not anybody else's. This is a union entirely different from the one previously described, I mean the "union in nature," because it implies no sort of conversion. This is what theologians call unio in persona, because it is essential to it that such transient or permanent accidents should have their being or their reality in that person. If it were not a human being it would more properly be called "union in the subject," but the philosophy would be the same in both instances.

It is this concept of union which Catholic doctrine applies to the mystery of the Incarnation with complete validity. It says that humanity has its being in God, through hypostatic union, as, for instance, my thoughts have their being in me, in my person, in persona. This is but the vaguest outline of a great mystery to be described more clearly hereafter.

The appropriation of transient and accidental phenomena by the permanent subject or person is, indeed, a fact of far-reaching consequences in the philosophy of created being. It points to a true distinction of reality in all created beings, personality being the complete and final mode of being, distinguishable from other factors of created reality even inside the same subject. For the moment this ontological law need not be explained more explicitly. In God alone there is no such possible distinction. Personality, persona, is to be taken in the sense of a substantial reality, not in the sense of a mere degree of higher dignity. It is the same thing as hypostasis or suppositum, Greek and Latin words respectively, which convey the idea of a complete and final individual being, possessing complete existence in the ontological order and complete responsibility in the moral order, if the being be a rational creature.

When Catholic theology says that the union of the Incarnation is in persona it means this: that the human element of Christ has been appropriated by a divine Person in that substantial sense, namely, that it entered into God's substantial Being, not into anything less. Catholic theology, being anxious to avoid any expression which might diminish the profound reality of that union, insists that we should say that this union is a union not only in persona but also in hypostasi or in supposito. God's substantial Being has taken unto itself human nature. It is not merely a communication of majesty and dignity on the part of God. It is a communication of personal, substantial, hypostatical being. This is the full meaning of the expression unio in persona when applied to the Incarnation.

St. Thomas gives us a very clear rendering of this ontological law which is of such supreme importance for our faith in the Incarnation:

> In a created person many accidental natures may find themselves together, as in the person of one man there are found quantity and quality. It belongs, however, properly to a divine Person, on account of his infinitude, that there should concur in him several natures, not only accidentally but substantially (III, q. 3, a. 1, ad 2).

The reason which is assigned by St. Thomas that a divine Person is able to communicate his Being to a finite individual nature is infinitude.

In the Incarnation the reality thus united in persona is not, as with us, an accidental or transient reality, but it is the permanent and substantial reality, the individual human nature of Christ. It is a nature composed of soul and body, as are all human natures. It is the constant teaching of Catholic theology that union of soul and body in Christ is the same as with other human beings. The profound difference is not in soul or body but in personality. In Christ soul and body come together to make a complete human nature, but they do not constitute a human personality, as is the case with us, the element of personality, if it may be so called, being supplied by the second Person of the Blessed Trinity. St. Thomas puts it thus:

> Through the union of soul and body in Christ there is not constituted a new hypostasis or person, but that compound enters into a preexisting person or hypostasis; and on this account it is said that union of soul and body in Christ is not of less efficacy than in us; because union with what is more noble, far from signifying loss of power or dignity, means gain (III, q. 2, a. 5, ad 1).

Here St. Thomas clearly insinuates a principle which belongs to the very essence of our faith in the Incarnation, namely, that something very real, very substantial, called created personality or hypostasis, which is found in all other human beings through the union of soul and body, is not found in Christ. Instead of it there is divine personality and divine hypostasis. No Catholic, to whatever school of metaphysics he may belong, can deny this replacement of something substantial in the order of being, where the lower created reality, the finite personality or hypostasis, is replaced by the infinite Personality or Hypostasis; otherwise he could not avoid falling into the error of Nestorius, who made the union between God and man in the Incarnation something merely accidental, and consequently admitted in Christ a double personality, a double hypostasis.

Nestorius, the Patriarch of Constantinople, was ready to profess every mode of union between the humanity in Christ and the divinity in him except the personal or hypostatic union. Obstinately he considered that there were really two individuals in Christ; though he professed his faith in a perfect and complete and admirable union between the two, this union or link could never be more than something accidental; so, according to him, it could never be said with literalness of truth that God was born of the Virgin or that God died on the Cross, he could see only and exclusively the human individual in the Christ who was born and died. That God was united with that individual at all times, in birth and in death, he, as a Christian, could not and did not deny, but in reality to him Christ meant two complete personalities, proceeding through life side by side, on parallel lines; though, of course, the divinity shed great luster on the humanity by its side.

Christian instinct, without any delay, revolted against this facile theology, and condemned it as heresy. The man who upheld the traditional faith was St. Cyril, Patriarch of Alexandria. In language whose accuracy has never been surpassed by later theologians, St. Cyril argues that to admit two personalities in Christ is to deny the Incarnation. The human nature in Christ, whatever the mode of union, is so united that it cannot be called a separate personality or hypostasis. The one personality is the God made man, and the union between man and God is not only moral but physical. This is why it can be said that God was born and that God died, because Christ's human nature is so completely appropriated by God that whatever is done in that human nature can be truly regarded as an act of God, just as the movement, say, of the human hand is considered to be the action of the man to whom the hand belongs. This view, as we know, was defined by the Council of Ephesus in 431 as the Catholic faith.

Nestorius never fell into the error of teaching a union in nature with regard to the Incarnation. He kept clearly asunder the divine and the human in Christ. But he was evidently incapable of grasping the philosophic notion of unio in persona, at least as a substantial union. For him an individual human nature was apparently the same thing as an individual human person. Though it may appear to be a difficult philosophical concept to distinguish between nature and person, Nestorius cannot be held excused, because, like the other theologians of his time, he had the clear guidance of Scripture and Catholic tradition, which are both express in declaring that God was made man, that God was born of the Virgin, that God shed his blood on the Cross. Such statements, which are the foundation of Christianity, imply at least philosophical consequence, namely, that Christ's human nature could not be called, and could not be, a complete person or hypostasis in the same sense in which other human beings are persons. Catholic theology could grant this much, that Christ's

Person or Hypostasis is a compound Person, in the sense that it exists in a duality of natures, the human and the divine; but the personal Being itself is entirely simple and one, as it is the personal Being of the second Person of the Trinity, which, besides being identified with the divine nature, is extended also to the human nature. On no account will Catholic theology allow us to say that Christ is a double person, and this distinction, far from being merely verbal, is the very foundation of the Christian faith.

3

The Perfection of the Union Between God and Man in the Incarnation

THE UNION BETWEEN THE HUMAN NATURE AND THE divine nature in the Incarnation is said by St. Thomas to be "the greatest of all unions": *maxima unionum*. But this does not in any way interfere with another doctrine of his, which is part of the Catholic faith, namely, that this union was brought about by a creative act of God, and that it is accordingly something created and not something increated. The reasoning of St. Thomas is clear: whatever begins in time is created: now the union of the Incarnation is not from eternity but it began in time: therefore it is something created. This is tantamount to saying that, not only was Christ's human nature created in time, but also the fact that it is united in Person with God is the effect of a divine action like creation.

The divine personality is, of course, increated, but that extension of itself to a finite nature is brought about by a creative act, in time. This act, like the entire acts of God *ad extra*, leaves God unchanged; all the change being in the creature. In the strict language of philosophy, it is a relation which is real in the creature, but merely logical, or, more clearly still abstract, in God. For the same reason we do not use promiscuously the words "unite" and "assume" in this matter of the Incarnation. We say truly that the human nature is united to the divine nature and that the divine nature is united to the human nature, but we do not say that the human nature assumed the divine nature. On the contrary, we profess explicitly that the divine nature assumed the human nature; all the activity of what might be called the "executive" in the work of the Incarnation being attributable to God alone; the human nature is entirely passive.

The perfection, then, of the union between the divine and the human in Christ is to be measured by the ontological oneness of the divine Person; that is to say, the attribute of oneness, which is a property of all being, is more perfect as the being is higher in the scale of reality. Oneness belongs to a divine Person as a transcending quality of infinite intensity. Now, as the personal Being of the Son of God is communicated to Christ's human nature, it follows that oneness is predicated of the subject, Christ, including the human and divine. In other words, the Person, Christ, has the same oneness as the eternal Word. So it is true to say, with St. Thomas, that Hypostatic Union is the greatest of all unions. St. Thomas puts it in this telling way:

> Man in a certain fashion is more in the Son (of God) than the Son is in the Father, for it is the same subsistence in what I call man and what I call Son of God, in the case of Christ, whilst the same subsistence is not of the Father and of the Son (III, q. 2, a. 9, ad 3).

More clearly, this means that whilst the Father does not share the personality of the Son because in the Trinity all three Persons are different, Christ's humanity shares the personality of the eternal Son of God.

From this it is clear that this union of the Incarnation could not be based primarily on sanctifying grace; such a union would be merely accidental and would not transcend the union of the other Saints with God. In the Incarnation the human nature is united with the divine nature in the Person of the Son. This is a union which is to sanctifying grace what a reality is to a mere similitude of itself, that is to say, union through sanctifying grace is only, in a finite way, a similitude of hypostatic union.

We have to admit, moreover, that in Christ, soul and body are united directly in the divine Person, so that there is not any sort of intermediary in that union, and the human nature in Christ is truly placed within the very life of God, so that it may be called a natural union. St. Thomas asserts that the personal union with God is natural to Christ's humanity because at no time was that human nature without the divine subsistence, nor is to be thought of at any time except as existing through divine subsistence. It is not as if Christ's humanity existed first independently and then was assumed into Hypostatic Union. In such hypothesis divine personality could not be said to belong naturally to Christ's humanity. Moreover, through the very laws of his conception the Child of Mary had to be the Son of God. St. Thomas says that it is natural to the human nature in Christ to be united to the Son of God on account of the mode of his origin, for he was thus conceived of the Holy Ghost that the same one was to be the natural Son of God and Son of Man.

Therefore there cannot be the question of any merit being the cause of such a union, for all the workings of Christ the Son of God are what they are on account of hypostatic union and therefore they could not merit hypostatic union; but hypostatic union is presupposed before there can be any question of merit: "The mystery of the

Incarnation is the principle of all merit, because from the fullness of Christ we all have received," says St. Thomas. Moreover, all merit is this, that the Spirit should be admitted to the fruition of God which is an act of the mind:

> But the union of the Incarnation as it takes place in personal being transcends the union of the mind of the blessed with God, which is brought about through an act of the one who enjoys the union of God. Therefore hypostatic union could never be the object of merit (III, q. 2, a. 11).

As a consequence of these considerations we have to profess that Christ is one, not only in the masculine gender, but even in the neuter gender: is *unus* and *unum*. He is one Person and one Being. He is not two beings united, much less is he two persons united, as Nestorius would have said. All we may say of Christ is this: that in his one Being there are differences of realities, there are in him the human and the divine. We may say that there are differences of qualities but not differences of beings.

As a last conclusion, and one that shows the perfection of the union in the Incarnation more clearly than all that has preceded, we have to say with St. Thomas that in Christ there is only "one Being," *unum esse*. The words of the Angelic Doctor are as follows:

> As human nature is joined unto the Son of God hypostatically (or in other words, personally) and not accidentally, it follows that on account of his human nature there does not accrue to him a new personal being (*novum esse personale*), but only a new relationship of the pre-existing personal being to the human nature; so that this person is said to exist (*subsistere*) not only ac-

cording to the divine nature but also according to the human nature (III, q. 17, a. 2).

In other words, Christ, though he be double in nature, human and divine, as truly and as literally as any man or any person, human, angelic or divine, says "I am," meaning thereby complete oneness of being. The duality of natures in him no more interferes with the literal truthfulness of this expression "I am" than the possession of various qualities different in kind in man interferes with his saying, in all exactness "I am." He may say "I am tired, I am well, I am content," but it is always the same pervading notion of complete oneness of personality: man has one being, one personal *esse*.

An important conclusion of St. Thomas is that Christ also (though in an infinitely real degree) has only one personal *Esse*. Christ would not say: "For this was *my humanity* born and came into the world, that I may give testimony to the truth," but he says: "For this was *I* born and came into the world that *I* may give testimony to the truth" (John 17:37). At no time does the duality of natures in him cause a duality of attribution, it is always one subject: "I say unto you," "I thirst," "Father, into thy hands I commit my soul." If there were really two beings in Christ, two *esse*, then Christ ought to speak of himself in the plural or he ought to differentiate within himself, as act and operations would proceed either from the human nature or the divine nature. There is never the least vestige of such duality in Christ's language right through the Gospels. The same subject, the pronoun "I" is made to bear realities and attributions of the most varied kind: "I and the Father are one," "I will raise him up in the last day."

These considerations are directly based on the very nature of the Incarnation. No Catholic could admit in Christ a double personal

being. It is not necessary for our faith to go beyond this simple statement of the oneness of personal Being in Christ; provided we admit
that his humanity is not a self-existing entity with independent hypostasis or personal being, we are within the limits of orthodoxy. But
in order to have a philosophic grasp of the terms of the dogmatic
definitions that is truly satisfying, no metaphysical system on being
is more helpful than the Thomistic one, which right throughout the
various branches of ontology teaches a real difference between nature
and personal being, except in God.

This distinction is again expressed as "a real difference between
essence and existence" in all created things: *Differentia realis inter esse
essentiae et esse existentiae.* This ontological law is taught and main-
tained by St. Thomas, not primarily in order to give a philosophical explanation of the hypostatic union in Christ with its oneness
of being, but in order to find an internal principle of differentiation
between the Creator and the creature. The Creator, *actus purus*, "pure
actuality," has no kind of duality in himself; nature and person, essence and existence are one and the same in him. In all finite beings
there is a real duality; even in the purest of spirits essence differs
from, existence, nature from person. With such metaphysical principles it becomes in a way understandable how the human nature in
Christ, though it is a reality not an abstraction, has no existence or
personal *esse* of its own, but the personal *esse* of the Word is extended
to it and makes it to be, and gives it existence. To contemplate this
oneness of divine Being which makes a human nature to exist in God
and through. God, is the blessedness of eternal life, according to the
words of Our Lord:

Father, I will that where I am, they also whom thou hast given me may be with me: that they may see my glory which thou hast given me, because thou hast loved me before the creation of the world (John 17:24).

4

The Function of the Divine Person in the Incarnation

It is the very essence of the mystery of the Incarnation that a divine Person should take an individual human nature into the participation of his own personal Being. The object of this chapter is to study more closely the nature of the function by which a divine Person assumes a created nature. That it should be able to do so is postulated by its own infinitude, as we have already said, quoting St. Thomas. The Angelic Doctor uses the expression *concursus naturarum*, "a flowing together of natures," in this connection. He says that:

> Several natures may come together in the divine personality, not indeed accidentally but substantially, on account of its infinitude. *Hoc autem est proprium divinae personae propter ejus infinitatem, ut fiat in ea concursus naturarum, non quidem accidentaliter, sed secundum subsistentiam* (III, q. 3, a 1, ad 1).

This function, then, has a twofold aspect: a causative and a terminative aspect.

The second aspect is, of course, the more important in the mystery of the Incarnation, as it constitutes the Incarnation. By the "terminative" aspect we mean this: that the divine Person is the term, the end, of the whole process of the Incarnation, as the human nature is united to it. To bring about this union requires an activity, a causation, on the part of God, which we call the "causative" aspect of the Incarnation. Now it is evident from all the principles of Catholic theology that all active causation, all efficacy *ad extra* is not done by one divine Person isolatedly, but by God in the totality of his Being. Therefore in the causative side of the Incarnation one divine Person is not more in evidence than the others. But the matter is quite different when we come to the terminative aspect. There it is true to say that one Person of the Trinity is the end of the process of the Incarnation to the exclusion of the others. The human nature in Christ is terminated, is joined unto the Second Person of the Trinity, not to the First or to the Third. This discrimination between Person and Person in the terminative aspect of the Incarnation is the very essence of the mystery; and with this aspect we are exclusively concerned when in this chapter we speak of the functions of the divine Person. What we said concerning the infinitude of the divine personality, as being the explanation of the possibility of the Incarnation, has to be applied to the terminative side of the mystery; on the executive side there is no more infinitude than in any other manifestation of God's creative power.

This termination of the human nature in the divine personality adds nothing to that personality; the whole gain is on the side of the human nature, just as grace in man, in the ordinary supernatural way, adds nothing to God. We must say, therefore, that owing to this termination of the human nature in the divine personality, humanity is truly predicated of the Second Person of the Trinity. God is made man through it. On account of it the Son of God, who is what he is from all eternity, is also Man from the time of his temporal birth. In this sense we may say that in the Person of Christ there is a secondary existence, besides the primary existence of the Word. The Word itself has an existence as the Son of Mary. This is entirely different from saying that Christ's humanity has a secondary existence besides the existence shared with the divine Person; in that sense we do not admit a secondary existence in Christ.

St. Thomas envisages a series of possibilities in the Incarnation, with regard to its terminative aspect, which are of supreme interest to the theologian, and which show how far Catholic theology is removed from considering the Incarnation as a limitation of God's personality in any way whatever. The personal union between the divine and the human nature in the Incarnation leaves the divine as unlimited and as free afterwards as it was before. Far from Catholic theology are thoughts which would circumscribe the unlimited. It is precisely the beauty of our theology to have been able to harmonize the philosophy of the *actus purus* with all the mercies of the Good Shepherd. As the union in the Incarnation is terminative, it leaves God in the full glory of his majesty, even then when he is said to be "meek and humble of heart" (Matt 11:29).

St. Thomas, then, makes the following hypothetical queries: Could every one of the divine Persons assume a human nature? Secondly, could several divine Persons assume one and the same human nature? Thirdly, could one divine Person assume several human natures? To all these queries he gives an affirmative reply, asserting that there is no kind of contradiction in such hypothetical positions.

It may be that under the circumstances the phraseology expressing the Incarnation would be altered, but the same principle—the terminative aspect of the Incarnation—would hold good in every one of these hypothetical instances.

With regard to the first hypothesis there can be no real difficulty. That either the Father or the Holy Ghost could be united with a human nature in the sense in which we understand such a union is, of course, obvious. The simplicity of the reasoning will surprise us. St. Thomas puts it thus:

> Whatever the Son can do, the Father can do, and the Holy Ghost can do; otherwise the three divine Persons would not have the same power. Now the Son has the power to be incarnated: therefore the Father and the Holy Ghost have that power also (III, q. 3, a. 5).

It would be superfluous to enter into further details and enquire how, in the case, for instance, of the Father being incarnated, the mystery would be expressed. We have to be satisfied with the general principle that it is within the power of every one of the three Persons of the Trinity to be united terminatively with a finite nature, as the three Persons have in common the causative power to bring about such a union.

The second hypothesis, that several divine Persons may assume one and the same human nature, presents, perhaps, a greater difficulty at first sight. Still St. Thomas sees no impossibility or contradiction in such a supposition. He argues from the fact that it is the very definition of the Trinity that three Persons should subsist in one nature:

> Now such is the characteristic of the Divine Persons that one does not exclude another from communicating in the same nature, but only in the same Person. *Est autem talis divinarum per-*

sonarum conditio, quod una earum non excludit aliam a commu-
niom ejusdem naturae, sed solum a communione ejusdem personae
(III, q. 3, a. 6).

In this matter of the Incarnation St. Thomas remarks that the rule is to follow more the character of the divine Person than the character of the human nature. As the possession of one divine nature by three Persons is in the character of the Trinity, there is no reason, according to the Angelical Doctor, why the possession of one human nature should not be in the character of the Trinity likewise. In this hypothesis, again, it would be logical to say that the three divine Persons are one man, as now it is logical to say that the three divine Persons are one God. In fact, St. Thomas pursues this parallel to all its consequences. The theology of the oneness of divine nature and Trinity of divine Persons could be extended *positis ponendis*, "by appropriate presupposition," to the oneness of human nature and the Trinity of divine Persons.

More interesting still is the third hypothesis which, in a way, is the contrary of the second. One divine Person would be able to assume two natures or, for the matter of that, an indefinite number of natures. Quite logically, Aquinas sees no inherent impossibility in such a theory. His fundamental principle is the infinitude of the divine Personality which can never be circumscribed. The words of St. Thomas are important:

We cannot say, therefore, that the divine Person assumed one human nature in such a fashion as to make it impossible for that Person to assume another nature, for it would mean in such a case that the Personality of the divine nature is circumscribed to the human nature, so that no other human nature could be assumed by that Personality, which is impossible; for the increated cannot be circumscribed by the created. Therefore, whether we consider the divine Person from the point of view of power, which is the cause of union, or from the point of view of Personality, which is the term of the union, our conclusions must be that the divine Person could assume another human nature numerically different from the one assumed (III, q. 3, a. 7).

Would it then mean that Christ would be called God-Man or would he be called God-Men? St. Thomas opines that he ought to be called God-Man just as he is at present:

> And hence, if the Divine Person were to assume two human natures, he would be called, on account of the unity of suppositum, one man having two natures. *Et ideo si persona divina assumeret duas naturas humanas, propter unitatem suppositi diceretur unus homo habens duas naturas humanas* (III, q. 3, a. 7, ad 2).

The great truth to be retained, as shown forth by such hypothetical theology, is this: the freedom of God in coming to man in the way he chose.

As a further contribution towards this theology of the divine freedom, St. Thomas takes the abstract case of God being considered, not as a Trinity, but as One, *ut Judaei intelligunt,* "according to the opinion of the Jews." Incarnation would still be possible; for in this Unitarian view the divine nature would be a person, a subsisting thing, and therefore, by reason of that personality, nature and person being entirely conterminous then in God, the Incarnation would be in principle on the same basis as it is now.

After conceding all this to God's freedom of choice, we come back with St. Thomas to the wonderful appropriateness and harmony of the Incarnation as it has taken place, one divine Person taking one human nature. Union with one human nature is sufficient, because through that one nature the Son of God became Man and became the all-sufficient source of grace and salvation for mankind. As the Incarnation is essentially God's work, making man into a new creature, it is the more appropriate that this work should be done through the Word, by whom all things were made at the beginning. The One who is born from the Father from all eternity is also born of a Virgin in time. Most fitting is it that we should become the sons of God by adoption through him who is the Son of God by nature.

Such considerations and many others of a like nature fill the books of Christian authors and the pages of the Christian Liturgies. They are the true Catholic sentiment towards the Incarnate God and they are the inspiration of the Christian poet and the Christian artist.

5

CHRIST'S HUMAN NATURE

MOST OF THE DIFFICULTIES PRESENTED BY THE DOCTRINE of the Incarnation center round the human nature which was assumed by the divine Person in the hypostatic union. In this wonderful union the Godhead, considered either as Person or as nature, remains, of course, quite unaltered and quite undiminished. Not so the human nature, as all that is real in the hypostatic union is so through some modification of that human nature, according to the principle that in all divine operation *ad extra* the relationship is a thing of reality in the creature, whilst in God it is only a logical thing.

It is the very essence of our faith in the Incarnation to admit that one, single, real, human nature has been assumed by the second Person of the Trinity into oneness of personality. It is not human nature in an abstract sense or human nature in its universality, but it is one, determined, single human nature that is part of Christ's personality through the Incarnation. Nothing that constitutes human nature is absent from the God-Man. There is in him body and soul, intelligence and senses, and in nothing is there any kind of mere appearance of humanity: this would be against the truth and dignity of the Incarnation. Wherein, then, does that single human nature which is Christ's differ from other human natures? Where must we look for that reality which makes the Incarnation to be, not a thing of fiction but a most sacred entity *in rerum natura*, "in the nature of things"? It is this: in contradistinction with all other human beings, Christ's human nature has no human personality. It is denuded of its human personality, in place of which it shares in the personality of the Son of God. This is the first and most indispensable element of the Incarnation, from which all other elements are derived. Thus it is certain that Christ's human nature has an immense measure of sanctifying grace and elicits acts of supernatural life of incalculable greatness and intensity; but these wonderful elements of the supernatural order do not constitute the hypostatic union, nor are they to be considered as a preparation for it. They are merely the results of a greater gift which transcends human consciousness, the communication by the Word of personal being to human nature.

Created and finite personality does not belong to Christ's human nature, it is absent from it. But this absence, though most real, is not a privation, being compensated for in an infinite measure by participation in the divine personality. At no time in the process of the Incarnation was Christ's humanity a person. It was only a nature. To assume a human person would have meant the destruction of that personality or it would have meant two personalities. The former alternative would have been contrary to God's ways, who never destroys what he creates. Nor would there have been any object in assuming a human personality as, of necessity; it would disappear at once in the hypostatic union. As St. Thomas says, in such hypothesis, "'The assumption would have been futile," *frustra esset assumpta* (III, q. 4, a. 2).

In the second alternative, the very essence of the hypostatic union would have been negated. It would mean Nestorianism. When, therefore, in the writings of the Fathers and other pious men we read such a phrase as "God took up man" we must understand it in the sense of a human nature without any human personality. Again to quote from the *Summa*:

Such phrases must be taken with pious understanding. *Hujus-modi locutiones non sunt extendendae tamquam propriae; sed pie sunt exponendae* (III, q. 4, a. 3, ad 1).

The all-pervading principle is this: "The human nature was taken up for this very end, that the Son of God be Man," *Assumptio terminata est ad hoc ut Filius Dei sit homo* (III, q. 4, a. 3, ad 1). The object of the Incarnation is not to give us a perfect human person, but to give us a God made man, in other words, a divine Person who is God and Man. Theoretically speaking, every rational creature could be hypostatically united to God. Likewise, theoretically speaking, any human nature could be thus united; but there are grave reasons of congruity why a human nature and not an angelical nature should be thus united, and also why the nature thus united should be of the seed of Adam. The congruity is to be found in the purpose of the Incarnation, which is the complete restoration of the fallen human race. A fallen angelic nature cannot be restored through the very laws of its spirit-will whilst man, in this life, may always be changed from evil to good. And it was the offspring of Adam that had sunk into sin. It shows infinite power and wisdom on the part of God in selecting this human nature from that race in such a wise that he should have all the reality of that nature, though he be infinitely removed from its stain of sin.

Human nature being a compound of spirit and matter, of soul and body, the question may be asked whether there be a priority, either of time or nature, in the process of the assuming. Was the soul of Christ united with the Divinity before that soul was united with its congenital body? Did it exist in personal union with the Word before the Word took flesh in the Virgin's womb? To give an affirmative answer to this would be heresy. It would mean a radical difference between Christ's conditions as Man and our conditions as men, as with the ordinary human being the soul does not exist at any time independently of its function as the *form* of the body, except, of course, after death. It may be said, however, with St. Augustine, that the Son of God assumed the lower elements of human nature through the higher elements in a kind of logical priority, as the higher elements in man are the appropriate reasons why man should be assumed. So it may be said that the soul was assumed through the intellect, and the body through the soul, in the sense in which we say that it was on account of the intellect that the soul was assumed and on account of the soul that the body was assumed. But this is merely a priority of reason. Through this we take it for granted that there could be no hypostatic union with an irrational being, or with dead or living matter which had no relationship with an intellectual being. But we do not mean that in the hypostatic union any part of the human nature was not most directly and immediately united with the divine Being. As St. Thomas puts it so clearly elsewhere:

> The word of God is said to be united with the flesh through the soul in the sense that it is through the soul that the flesh belongs to the human nature which the Son of God resolved to take unto himself. But not in the sense that the soul is the binding medium between the two united realities. *Verbum Dei dicitur unitum carni mediante anima, inquantum caro per animam pertinet ad huma-*

nam naturam, quam Filius Dei assumere intendebat; non autem ita quod anima sit quasi medium ligans unita (III, q. 1, a. 3, ad 1).

For this reason in the *triduum*, "three days," of the Lord's death, Christ's body in the sepulcher remained perfectly and completely united with the divine personality. Moreover, again according to St. Thomas, Christ's personality in death was not broken up as is the ordinary human personality at death; it remained in its entirety. All that happened was that the two elements of his human nature, the soul and the body, were separated, but the personality itself remained in its entirety. The whole Christ was in the tomb and the whole Christ was in Limbo. Or again, in the words of Aquinas:

> When death severed the union of the soul with the body, the whole Christ remained, but his whole human nature did not remain. *Soluta unione animae et corporis per mortem, remansit totus Christus, sed non remansit humana natura in sua totalitate* (III, q. 52, a. 3, ad 2).

In this matter of the immediateness of the union between the divine Person and the human nature we must always bear in mind that the whole object of the Incarnation is, as already said, oneness of personality. Everything is subservient to this great end:

> It is a personal union wherein the assumption is terminated, not a union of nature, which springs from a conjunction of parts. *Unio personalis est ad quam terminatur assumptio; non autem unio naturae, quae resultat ex conjunctione partium* (III, q. 6, a. 5, ad 3).

The Incarnation remains perfect even when, as in the death of Christ, nature is no longer perfect, that is to say, when its elements are no longer perfectly united.

6

THE SANCTIFYING GRACE OF CHRIST

ALTHOUGH IT BE ONE OF THE PIVOTAL PRINCIPLES OF the Catholic theology on the Incarnation that hypostatic union is not *in natura* but *in persona*, it does not follow from this that Christ's nature remains unchanged, even as nature, under the hypostatic union. It is, on the contrary another most important element of our doctrine of the Incarnation that Christ's human nature, and chiefly Christ's human soul, is transmuted under the hypostatic union to a degree inconceivable to us. Although, as is so often said, hypostatic union is essentially this, that Created personality in Christ does not exist, but only increated personality, and that therefore Christ's human element has no personality of its own, it does not follow that the human nature thus assumed unto divine personality remains untouched by the fire of the divinity. On the contrary it is made as divine as possible, as divine a nature as a created being can possibly become. This is done through sanctifying grace:

> As (in Christ) with the oneness in person there remains the distinction of natures, the soul of Christ is not divine through its

essence; therefore it was necessary that it should be made divine through participation, which is, through grace (III, q. 7, a. 1, ad 1).

In other words, it is in strict accordance with Catholic theology to say that when God assumed a human nature into the oneness of person it was his intention to assume that nature not only in its low-liness and infirmities but also in all the glory of which that nature is capable. Most likely it would imply contradiction that the created nature should be assumed hypostatically *in persona* without that na-ture, as nature, being elevated in the supernatural order to the highest possible degree; for it would really be a profound lack of harmony in the Person of Christ. Oneness of person in two natures seems to necessitate the closest conceivable approximation of the human na-ture to the divine. This is done, as already said, through habitual or sanctifying grace with all its gifts and ramifications. It was no doubt this desire to see Christ's human nature divinized that led to the ex-aggeration of the Eutychian heresy, which denied in Christ the dual-ity of natures and which taught that the human nature was absorbed by the divine nature. It is certainly necessary to bring Christ's human nature into closest proximity with the divine nature, otherwise, as al-ready insinuated, there would be a real hiatus in Christ's personality. Oneness of person is not the same as oneness of nature; still it must bring about complete harmony between the two natures thus united in one hypostasis. The doctrine of sanctifying grace gives all Eutyches could have desired and saves us from the extravagances of the immer-sion of a created being in an increated being.

St. Thomas is very insistent on one point: sanctifying grace in the soul of Christ is not a preparation for hypostatic union but a result of it; the underlying thought being this, that no amount of grace could entitle a creature to be assumed hypostatically. But, once assumed, the created nature, even in its finite reality, is a harmonious part of the divine Person through gifts whose proportions we do not know, but which come under the name of grace. To add to these considerations the further observation that the soul of Christ had to perform operations of knowledge and love, of supreme excellency, worthy of the nature of the Son of God, though it be his secondary nature, is to express the same idea in other words. Since grace is essentially the source and the root of such operations, Christ's office as mediator between God and man also postulates the presence of sanctifying grace in his human nature. He is to the human race the source of all grace: but this, again, is only a development of the central fact that Christ's soul must be harmonized with Christ's divinity, for this harmony is to be considered in its full extent not only of quality but also of action. Christ's human nature works in one Person with the Godhead for the salvation of mankind. In the language of Catholic theology, Christ's human nature is the instrument of the divinity in working out man's salvation.

More will be said later concerning this supernatural instrumentality; Christ's humanity is a living instrument closely united with divinity, therefore it was right that it should be endowed with all the vitalities requisite to give life to the world. Such vitalities are called grace. It may be said, then, that hypostatic union, strictly defined, transcends all experience and consciousness. It is essentially entitative. Through it the human nature is divine in the infinite sense of the word. But hypostatic union at once causes gifts which come under experience and consciousness: they are of the spiritual order; through them Christ's humanity is experimentally conscious of its union with the divine Person. Christ received the fullness of grace the moment that hypostatic union was accomplished. By this we mean that he received grace, not only in full measure, but in full development; that is to say, Christ's soul, from the first moment of its existence, was given the clear Vision of God and the immediate fruition of God in the fullest possible degree. Christ, we say, has been a *comprehensor*, "understander,"from the first moment of his existence, seeing God face to face and tasting the sweetness of the divine Essence as do the elect in heaven. To neglect or to forget this tremendous fact would lead to most disastrous heresy in our study of Christ's psychology. Christ, however, is said to have been a *viator*, "traveler," at the same time, i.e. one who had work still to do here on earth, who had to walk the dreary road of mortal life, of mortal suffering and of death. If we are to decide whether Christ possessed and exercised definite virtues or was endowed with special gifts we must examine each point in the light of this twofold truth, that Christ at the same time was *comprehensor* and *viator*.

It could not, then, be said that Christ possessed the gift of theological faith in its strict acceptation, because the theological virtue of faith means the obscurity of the object, a condition entirely incompatible with the state of clear vision in which Christ's soul found itself. Similarly, the theological virtue of hope could not be predicated of Christ in its strict meaning, as hope, considered technically, implies an element of arduousness; the thing for which we hope, theologically speaking, is such as not to be in our grasp as yet. Now Christ in his Person possessed God so fully and completely that there was no danger of his ever being estranged from God. This does not mean that Christ did not expect certain manifestations of the Father's goodness in his favor in the future, such as his glorification and his triumph. But these advantages were rather expected than hoped for, because they were bound to come to him through the very fact that he was the Son of God. The gifts of the Holy Ghost are attributed to Christ with perfect accuracy of language because they are permanent perfections of the human soul belonging to the state of *viator* as well as to the state of *comprehensor*. The prophecy of Isaiah is applied directly to Christ's human soul:

> And there shall come forth a rod out of the root of Jesse: and a flower shall rise up out of his root. And the spirit of the Lord shall rest upon him; the spirit of wisdom and of understanding, the spirit of counsel and of fortitude, the spirit of knowledge and of godliness. And he shall be filled with the spirit of the fear of the Lord (Isa 11:1-3).

The great distinction in the matter of grace is between *gratia gratum faciens* "sanctifying grace," and *gratia gratis data*, "charism." This latter is the power given to man "for the manifestation of faith and supernatural doctrine," *Ad fidei et spiritualis doctrinae manifestationem*. This grace, or series of graces, was possessed by Christ in its fullness, according to St. Thomas, as it is Christ's mission to manifest to men the truth of God.

Fullness is the first quality of Christ's grace: *Vidimus eum plenum gratiae et veritatis*, "We beheld him full of grace and truth" (John 1:14). The Scriptures abound in expressions to the same effect. Christ has grace as fully as it can be possessed and his grace suffices for all the possible needs of the human race in the order of grace. But it is not as easy for us to understand how that grace had absolute fullness, for we must still think it possible, absolutely speaking, that the created grace could have been greater. The wisest thing said in this matter is found in the *Summa*:

> Although divine power can make something better and greater
> than this habitual grace of Christ, it cannot make anything which
> is ordered towards a greater good than personal union with the
> only-begotten of the Father. The measure of (Christ's) grace is
> such as to correspond adequately with that union according to
> the definition of divine wisdom (III, q. 7, a 12, ad 2).

This expression, *secundum definitionem divinae sapientiae*, "according
to the definition of divine wisdom," is no doubt the only safe formula
for our guidance in this most mysterious matter.

So we do not say that Christ's human grace was infinite in the
absolute sense of that word. St. Thomas gives for the reason of this
the obvious fact that Christ's human soul, being a creature, had only
finite capacity. A certain infinitude, however, may be attributed to
Christ's grace, because it is such as to be inexhaustible, so that an
endless series of created beings can find in Christ's grace the source
of their own. For all these reasons it is evident that Christ's grace
could not receive any true augmentation as it was in its full perfection
from the very beginning, and Christ in the matter of grace was not a
viator; he was a *comprehensor*; he was *in statu termini*, "in the state of
completion." These theological terms are universally received in the
schools. Man here on earth is said to be a *viator*, a wayfarer; in heaven
he is an "understander," a *comprehensor*, and he has reached the goal,
the *status termini*.

Such growth in grace as that of which the Gospels tell means
progression in the sense of ever new manifestation of the grace that
was in him: "And Jesus advanced in wisdom and in age and grace
with God and men" (Luke 2:52). Such words are easily compatible with
the hidden realities of Christ's personality, described in this chapter.

The gradual development of the new-born Savior from Childhood to Manhood was natural to him. So likewise it was natural that such works of grace as depended on his human power of the natural kind should also evince gradual development.

7

THE GRACE OF CHRIST IN HIS
OFFICE AS HEAD OF THE CHURCH

CHRIST'S HEADSHIP OVER ALL CREATION IS PART OF HIS
position as God-Man and as Redeemer of the world. In this
larger sense the headship of Christ means supreme authority over all
creatures; but a more restricted and precise meaning may be attached
to the metaphor of the head in connection with Christ: he is the head
of the Church:

> And he hath subjected all things under his feet and hath made
> him head over all the church. Which is his body and the fullness
> of him who is filled all in all (Eph 1:22).

In this passage St. Paul speaks of that double headship. There is first
that superiority over all things—"And he has subjected all things under his feet," and there is then the special relationship of Christ to his
Church. Christ is the head and the Church is the body. The same idea
is expressed in the Epistle to the Colossians:

> And he is before all: and by him all things exist. And he is the head

of the body, the church: who is the beginning, the firstborn from the dead, that in all things he may hold the primacy (Col. 1:17).

In this chapter we are speaking of Christ as the head in the sense of the development of created grace in Christ's personality of which there was question in the last chapter, i.e. of the restricted headship of Christ, and of his relationship with the Church which is called his body.

It is important for the clarity of theological thought to keep asunder these two interpretations of Christ's headship, for not all things that are predicated of his headship in the universal sense could be predicated of his headship in the more restricted sense. The dominant idea of the headship in the vaster meaning is this: that Christ through the hypostatic union is infinitely superior to all creatures: "He is before all and by him all things consist" (Col 1:17). On the other hand the dominant thought of the headship of the second order is that Christ, with all his wealth of grace, is still part of one organic whole—himself and his Church—and he is head because the life that is in him is communicated in its "identity," *Specie specialissima*, to the Church.

Headship over the Church means essentially that Christ in his humanity has power to communicate to the souls of the redeemed the kind of supernatural life that is in himself, to communicate it in its very essence, homogeneously, identically. For this is expected of Christ as the head of the Church, that he should give his own grace to that Church. By grace we mean, of course, the whole supernatural order in all its ramifications, in the sense of spiritual qualities of every kind possessed by rational creatures. God, considered in his divinity, produces creatures more and more conformable to himself, bearing greater and closer resemblances to the divine nature; but the resemblances will never be perfect; they are only analogical, as theologians say. Now we expect that Christ as head of the Church will communicate to it his own created graces, not analogically but univocally, so that they are identical with those that are in himself, though there be a difference in degree.

From this we see that the more universal headship is prior to the more restricted one. It is because Christ as God, as the First-born of all things, has redeemed men that his second headship is possible. He is given as the head to those who are redeemed by his blood. As head in the restricted sense he is not a "Redeemer," but a "Vivifier": as head in the larger sense he is a "Redeemer" who has reconciled all things unto the Father.

The question now arises whether Christ in his humanity can truly fulfill this office of head, in the restricted sense. Is it possible for Christ's human nature to carry out that universal vivifying of the souls of men which is expressed by the metaphor of the head of the body? The answer of St. Thomas is emphatically in the affirmative:

> To give grace or the Holy Ghost belongs to Christ in fullness of authority according to his Godhead, but instrumentally it belongs to him also in his Manhood, as far as his Manhood was the instrument of his divinity. And thus his actions through the power of the divinity brought us salvation in the sense that they caused grace in us. And this in a twofold way: first by merit, and secondly through a kind of efficiency (III, q. 8, a. 1, ad 1).

Here St. Thomas distinguishes between the meritoriousness of Christ's acts and their efficiency. Christ in his humanity causes grace, not only through his ethical merit, but in a sort of executive way of the real physical order. This St. Thomas explains with his well-known concept of the divine instrumentality of which more will be said hereafter. So St. Thomas admits in a general way that it is not beyond the power of a created being, such as Christ's humanity, to be the head of the Church in the restricted sense of real vivifying. Some theologians denied this power to Christ's humanity on the ground that thus the whole work of the Redemption would be attributed, not to the God Incarnate, but to his humanity. But such an objection misses the point. When we speak of Christ's headship in this restricted sense we do not speak of Redemption, we speak of grace, the formal element of sanctification, which makes all the members of the Church to be holy; and we say that it is in the power of Christ's humanity to communicate such grace. We presuppose the Redemption as being the remote cause of all grace and as being essentially the work of the God-Man. In other words, hypostatic union explains Redemption, whilst Christ's finite grace as man is the explanation of the headship in the restricted sense.

As a further conclusion, St. Thomas says that the grace through which Christ is properly called the head of the Church is not directly hypostatic union, but his created grace as man:

> [And, therefore, the same is in accordance with the essence of the personal grace, by which the soul of Christ is justified: and his grace, according to which He is the Head of the Church, justifying others.] *Et ideo eadem est secundum essentiam gratia personalis, qua anima Christi est justificata, et gratia ejus, secundum quam est caput Ecclesiae justificans alios* (III, q. 8, a. 5).

Moreover, St. Thomas considers Christ's grace in this final aspect as being the cause of our grace on account of his supreme eminence.

There is in Christ such power of grace that it illumines all those whom it touches with its own rays. The created grace itself that is in Christ is communicated to us as light is communicated by the sun, having such power of excellence that it can perform what the grace of no ordinary saint could possibly achieve, however intense that grace might be. Eminence of grace in Christ does not mean difference in kind from our grace, but it means supreme power of communicability.

This influence of Christ as the head of the Church must be taken in the vastest sense possible. Not only the soul of Christ, but the whole Christ, soul and body, radiates grace. And this grace affects the whole man, soul and body; the resurrection of the flesh is as much Christ's work as head of the Church as are justification and sanctification. The flesh of Christ and the blood of Christ in the Eucharist are inexhaustible sources of grace to the Church.

It may be asked how mankind, taken in its universality, participates in the benefits of Christ's headship, considered in the more restricted meaning. It is clear, of course, that Christ is the head of all men living and dead, in the more universal acceptation of the term headship. The question asked here is more limited: can it be said that all men are under the influence of Christ as the source of life and that Christ is the head of all men, not only the head of the Church? St. Thomas gives an affirmative answer to this query. In order to do so he establishes a fourfold division of men and their potentialities with regard to Christ's headship.

There are firstly the elect in heaven, gathered from the whole human race. They are fully and completely members of Christ.

Secondly, there are those men here on earth who have faith in Christ, a faith informed by charity. They are members of Christ, indeed, but not completely, because they do not yet receive the total influence of the life of Christ, such totality being found in heaven only.

Thirdly, there are those who have faith, but whose faith is not informed by charity. They are in the state of mortal sin. They are members of Christ, they are under his supernatural influence through the very fact that they possess faith, but they are the sick and wounded members of Christ's body.

Fourthly, there is in all men a direct potentiality to be admitted to Christ's grace in all its degrees. This potentiality comes, no doubt, from the deeper fact that all men without exception are redeemed by Christ, and all men have that freedom of will which is the indispensable prerequisite for grace. St. Thomas considers this most real potentiality to be sufficient in order to give validity to the assertion that all men are under Christ's headship, taking this headship in the most technical meaning. He excludes, however, from the benefits of that headship all the "reprobate," those who die outside God's friendship. In no sense would these be members of Christ, even by a remote possibility: Christ is their head only as the Lord and Judge of all creatures.

This doctrine of the headship of Christ may be extended further and made to embrace, not only the elect of all the human race but also the heavenly spirits. The argument of St. Thomas reads thus:

> It is clear that angels and men are made for one and the same end: the glory of the divine fruition. Therefore the mystical body of Christ consists not only of men but also of angels. Now of all that multitude Christ is the head (III, q. 8, a. 4).

That Christ in himself as Man possessed such life as to make him the king of the angels is evident from the fact that he is the greatest *comprehensor*, that he is nearer to God than any creature, that he receives the gifts of God more plentifully than all angels and men together.

A doubt might be suggested as to the nature of that *influxus* which would justify the role of headship with regard to the angels. Are we to say that the grace of the angels comes to them in the same way as the Church's grace comes from Christ? It is, of course, by no means opposed to Catholic theology to maintain that the heavenly spirits might have received their graces *intuitu Christi*, "on account of the Christ" who was from eternity predestinated to be head of the universe, even as Adam received his grace *intuitu Christi*. But this is not necessary in order to establish the spiritual headship of Christ over the angels.

St. Thomas puts the matter in this noncommittal phrase: *De ejus (Christi) influentia non solum homines recipiunt sed etiam angeli*, "Not only men receive his (Christ's) influence, but also the angels" (III, q. 8, a. 4). What this influence is, the Angelical Doctor does not decide. But it seems evident that even angelic life must be deeply modified through the presence of the Son of Man at the right hand of God in glory; so St. Thomas had no difficulty in explaining the following text as meaning the headship of Christ in the restricted sense:

> Which he wrought in Christ, raising him up from the dead and setting him at his right hand in the heavenly places. Above all principality and power and virtue and dominion and every name that is named, not only in this world, but also in that which is to come (Eph. 1:20, 21).

This headship of Christ is, of course, incommunicable to the saints however full of grace, and no minister of Christ, lavish though his endowment of spiritual powers might be, could ever be called the head of the Church. In external administration Bishops are the heads of their flocks; the Pope is truly the head of the universal Church *tempore sui Pontificatus*, "in the time of his Pontificate" (III, q. 8, a. 6). But such headship is very relative; it has none of that universality of time, space, power and grace which is Christ's exclusive glory.

8

The Knowledge of the Incarnate Son of God

THERE IS NO PROVINCE OF CHRISTOLOGY IN WHICH THE consequences and the conclusions from the principles of hypostatic union are made more clearly manifest than in the theology of the knowledge of the Son of God. In this matter the only safe line of action for the theologian is to admit, even to the point of bewildering excellency and extremity, all that is contained in the general truth that Christ is supreme in all things, and that to his knowledge there is really no limit.

It is one of the great merits of the Christology of St. Thomas that he never hesitated, from any mental bewilderment, to attribute to Christ every conceivable form of knowing power. This he does with a full consciousness of the human and finite conditions of Christ's soul. Where it is necessary he attributes to Christ's knowledge certain modifications postulated by his humanity, though, to tell the truth, he never seems to admit any real limits to Christ's knowledge. In this St. Thomas differs profoundly from the moderns, at least from such moderns as are not under the influence of Catholic theology. St. Thomas sees no merit, no beauty, no power of salvation or of edification in a Christ whose mind is impoverished by ignorance or distracted by doubt. His Christ is essentially at the head of all creation and he is a helper and a savior because in him is all reality and all truth.

Considering Christ as a Person we have to predicate of him four distinct classes of knowledge. Firstly, there is in him the infinite knowledge, as Word of God. Secondly, in his humanity, there is the knowledge which is technically called *Visio Dei beata*, "the blessed Vision of God." Thirdly, there is in him, with such modifications as are postulated by the constitutional elements of the human intellect, all the knowledge which belongs to the disembodied spirits—its technical name is *scientia infusa*, "infused knowledge"—the knowledge which is poured into the mind by God. The fourth kind of knowledge that is in the Person of Christ, which is the third kind in his human nature, is the knowledge which comes from the activities of the *intellectus agens*, "agent intellect," that mysterious power in man which enables him to acquire knowledge daily, more and more, *ad infinitum*, "to infinity."

In this chapter we are not, of course, concerned with the first class of knowledge, which is the very essence of the eternal Word, except in so far as we make the Word in the Person of Christ the measure of human and created knowledge in the sense that between Christ's created intellect and increated intellect there is a sort of harmony. We have already said, when treating of sanctifying grace, that there must be supernatural harmony and a sort of proportion between Christ's human nature and Christ's divine nature in the hypostatic union; so likewise, in this matter of knowledge, as the Person called Christ is divine Wisdom Incarnate, the human element of that Person must share in eternal Wisdom to an extent no created intellect can fathom. Otherwise it would not be true to say that eternal Wisdom has appeared in the flesh.

Christ possessed the clear vision of God from the very beginning of his human existence. That glory which comes to the elect as the end of all their merit—the clear vision of God, face to face—was Christ's from the first moment he was conceived in the Virgin's womb. Christ was a *comprehensor*, one who sees God in the clarity of unveiled vision, at all times. That glorification of his Person which came to him at the Resurrection did not affect his intellect, as that intellect was always in a state of glory through the very laws of his being. Christ's mortal state, or as it is called, Christ's passibility, had its seat, not in his intellect but in his bodily senses

Many valid reasons can be advanced in order to establish this great *placet*, "vote of approval," of Catholic theology. St. Thomas in his *Summa* refers us again to Christ's role of head of the Church in order to show the necessity for Christ to have beatific vision in the most excellent way and as an attribute belonging to him by birthright. The clear vision of God, he says, is man's supernatural end. It is man's final goal of happiness. To this goal man is brought by Christ; it is necessary, therefore, that he himself should be in that happy state into which he leads all his elect. The personal union belongs entirely to the ontological order of things and does not make the soul of Christ happy in an experimental way. This is done by a created gift: the clear vision of God. Says St. Thomas:

> It was necessary that there should be in the human nature of Christ a certain blessedness through which his soul is established in the last end of human nature. *Oportuit in natura humana Christiesse quamdam beatificationem creatam per quam anima ejus in ultimo fine humanae naturae constitueretur* (III, q. 9, a. 2, ad 2).

Before proceeding with the inquiry as to the possible extent of that blessed vision in Christ's soul, we may with St. Thomas at once consider the relation between Christ's beatific vision and the other kinds of created knowledge in that soul. The question which arises is this: did beatific vision in Christ's intellect render inferior forms of knowledge superfluous? The emphatic answer of Catholic theology, voiced by St. Thomas, is that, far from rendering other forms of knowledge superfluous, beatific vision postulates them.

So we come at once to infused knowledge: *scientia infusa*. In this matter of Christ's knowledge we apply to him principles of theology which have an independent value and which do not belong exclusively to the theology of the Incarnation. In this portion of theology of the Incarnation, we only apply to Christ the general doctrines concerning the clear vision of God by created minds; there is a special tractate in all our books of theology on beatific vision; likewise there is abundant speculation in our books of theology concerning the *scientia infusa*, chiefly in connection with angelic life; here we only apply to Christ what we know from other sources of theology.

The position of Catholic theology is this: that a created spirit receives from God knowledge in measure more and more abundant in accordance with his own perfection. This knowledge is not acquired, it is concreated with the spirit; it is his natural equipment; it is essentially an attribute of the angels. Now, did Christ also possess that class of knowledge? St. Thomas is emphatic in attributing it to him for this reason that, being the head of all creation, his intellectual powers had to be filled with every kind of light; they had to reach all those heights for which they had any potentiality. Now, it is not beyond the human intellect to be thus endowed, at least through a supernatural, interference of God; though such knowledge be congenital only to the purest spirits, it may be possessed by the human soul through a special operation of God. In other parts of theology it is admitted that human souls which reach heaven, besides enjoying beatific vision, are also granted a participation in this angelic mode of knowing.

The question, then, arises, what is the relationship between the two visions, the vision in God and the vision in the angelic light? The answer is simple in the extreme: that created angelic knowledge beholds reality in itself as it is, *extra Deum*, "outside of God," whilst beatific vision beholds reality exclusively *sub specie Divinitatis*, "in God, as part of God." Over and over again our theologians make use of the poetical expression of St. Augustine who divides between *scientia matutina* "morning knowledge," and *scientia vespertina*, "evening knowledge." By matutinal knowledge the Bishop of Hippo means seeing things in God; by the evening knowledge he means beholding created realities in themselves. It is then considered supreme perfection in God's ordering of the intellectual universe that created minds should find in God what they have seen outside God, and that, on the other hand, they should see realized in themselves in a created state those ideals which are the very life of God. So St. Thomas says of Christ what in a way he would say of all blessed spirits that are in heaven, I mean the human souls:

> In Christ with the blessed knowledge (of vision) there remains the infused knowledge (of angelic nature), not as if the latter were a way to the blessed vision, but as finding in the blessed vision its confirmation. *In Christo simul cum scientia beatitudinis manet scientia indita, non quasi via ad beatitudinem, sed quasi per beatitudinem confirmata* (III, q. 9, a. 3, ad 2).

A very interesting point in theology can be made out of the question whether one already so richly endowed possessed also acquired human knowledge, whether he was a real learner as other men are learners. It is one of the few disputed theories of theology about which St. Thomas makes a clear retractation of the opinions he held in his younger days. In the Summa he says that in former works he was of opinion that Christ did not learn in a human way; but maturer reflection led him to the conclusion that "acquired human knowledge," (*scientia acquisita*) is to be predicated of Christ as truly as of other men. In all matters of Christ's knowledge he is guided by the following considerations: all potentialities and all powers in Christ's humanity must receive their full realization and actuation; in Christ, as in other men, there is the *intellectus agens*, it belongs to the very essence of human nature. Now it is the special office of the *intellectus agens* to enable men to learn, to acquire knowledge through the multitudinous channels of observation. Such a power could not be dormant in Christ, he used it to its fullest extent but always in a natural and congenital fashion. The workings of the *intellectus agens* depend on the gradual developments of the human organism, so it is to be admitted that even in Christ that power had to await the ripenings of the organism; but at every period of his development as child and adolescent Christ with his human faculties was able, through natural keenness of perception, to investigate nature and its mysteries.

It is to be noted that St. Thomas very wisely makes this portion of theology center round the psychological principle of the *intellectus agens*. Sometimes this last mode of knowledge in Christ is called his "experimental knowledge" (*scientia experimentalis*). St. Thomas himself occasionally makes use of the expression. The idea might be suggested that by experimental knowledge is meant nothing else than a contact with the physical world, either in pain or joy. This of course is not excluded, but it does not constitute the *scientia acquisita*; "invention" is a word which would more truly represent the scope of that special kind of knowledge in Christ. This is why I say that St. Thomas was wise in studying the range of Christ's natural intellectual powers from the angle of the *intellectus agens*. How with the possession of all knowledge a priori this acquired knowledge is a real enrichment of Christ's humanity has already been explained, at least in principle. It is a perfection of the mind to be able to approach truth not only in one way but in many ways.

We come now to the very interesting results of Catholic theological speculations concerning the extent of Christ's created knowledge in the three spheres just described. Here St. Thomas is truly majestic. He starts from the principle, which he considers to be beyond contradiction, that whatever in any way has relationship with Christ's Person and Christ's office as Redeemer of mankind, as Head of the Church, as King of the universe, must be known to Christ, not only in his divinity but in his humanity. This means practically infinitude of knowledge. St. Thomas finds no difficulty in attributing such infinitude of knowledge to Christ's intellect; his notions concerning infinitude make it possible for him to lay down such rules for Christ's created mind. St. Thomas says that it is not possible for a created mind, even the mind of Christ, to comprehend the infinite infinitely, that is to say, from all parts and all aspects, but it is possible for a finite mind to behold infinitude in a given direction; thus it would be possible for a created intellect to see at a glance even an infinite number of human acts, because such an infinitude is limited to one class of reality. But no created intellect would comprehend God completely, because God is, so to speak, infinite in every direction.

The practical aspect of this wonderful theology is, of course, obvious. Christ in his lifetime had present before his mind his whole vast work of redemption with all its incredible ramifications in nature and in grace. A difficulty is traditionally made at this stage of theology. It arises from the text in St. Mark 13:32:

> But of that day or hour no man knoweth, neither the angels in heaven, nor the Son, but the Father.

There is, however, the constant sense of Catholic Doctors that Christ in his humanity did know the hour of the end of the world. Many Doctors, and St. Thomas with them, seem to think that with this expression Christ merely meant that he was not expected to make known the mysterious hour to the Apostles. One other explanation that could be given is this, that the act could not be known except by one actually comprehending God. This full comprehension of God we do not attribute to Christ's human intellect. But it is possible for God to reveal in another way the mysteries of his will. To Christ's human nature certainly that hour was revealed, but we may say that he knew it neither in beatific vision nor in the *scientia infusa* and much less in the *scientia acquisita*, but through some special revelation exclusive to himself. But this is a mere suggestion.

In this matter of Christ's created knowledge St. Thomas applies a principle whose usefulness he presses in other matters in his treatise on the Incarnation. Did Christ receive knowledge from a creature, human or angelic? Did he, for instance, learn from his blessed Mother or, to quote a more remarkable example, did the angel who comforted him in his agony in the garden teach or show anything new? St. Thomas quite consistently attributes to such created interventions concerning the Person of Christ a merely ministerial value. The Son of God in order to show forth the genuineness of his human nature accepted such ministrations, though they were not necessary to him. With all the Fathers, St. Thomas views those ministrations on the part of creatures to Christ as condescensions on his part. Let us quote St. Thomas:

> That comforting on the part of the angels was not by way of teaching but in order to show forth the reality of his human nature. So Bede says: "As an evidence of the two natures, angels are said to have ministered to him and to have comforted him. The Creator indeed is not in need of the help of his creature, but having become Man, as for our sakes he was made sad, so for our sakes he was comforted (III, q 12, a. 4, ad 1).

In other words, it was Christ's intention that the faith in his Incarnation should be strengthened in us.

9

The Power of Christ

THE WONDERFUL CONCLUSIONS OF CATHOLIC THEOLOGY concerning the knowledge of Christ in his humanity lead one naturally to inquire, what are the powers, one might say, the executive, corresponding with such knowledge. It must be admitted, however, from the very outset, that much less is granted by theology to Christ's humanity in this matter of power than in the case of knowledge. The reason of this is twofold. Firstly, the exercise of power seems to belong more immediately to the Person than to nature, whilst knowledge belongs more immediately to nature than to the Person. In order that all things should be true that Christ himself has said concerning his power it is not necessary to make those distinctions between the two natures which are indispensable in the matter of knowledge. Thus, when Christ says that all power is given to him in heaven and on earth it is sufficient to remember that he is God Incarnate, a divine Person, subsisting in two natures. He is omnipotent because he is God-Man. There is really no need, speaking absolutely, for his humanity to have exceptional powers of executive, though there is an absolute need for the intellectual faculties of Christ's humanity to be at their fullest possible degree of development. It is enough for Christ's humanity to be united hypostatically with the Word. As such it shares *per communicationem idiomatum*, "through the communication of properties," in omnipotence.

Secondly, there is a profound difference in the finite and created sphere of reality between knowledge and executive power. Much knowledge is given to creatures of things which they would never be able to carry out by themselves. It is God's exclusive property that his infinite knowledge should be at the same time theoretical and practical, in the sense that whatever he knows to be feasible he can do. Quite logically, then, this question of our Lord's power as a separate point of theology is asked in connection, not with Christ's Person, for as Person he is evidently omnipotent, but in connection with his humanity. St. Thomas speaks even more exclusively "of the power of the soul of Christ" (*de potentia animae Christi*), than he had spoken before of the knowledge of the soul of Christ. Quite definitely his answer is negative to the query whether Christ's soul possesses omnipotence, except in the sense of *communicatio idiomatum*. Nor does he in this matter concede to Christ's soul, considered in itself, that partial infinitude in power which he granted so liberally in the matter of knowledge:

> There is no kind of matter for the knowledge of which at least of some sort (*aliqualiter*) an infinite faculty of knowing is required, though a certain (i.e. comprehensive) mode of knowing is the property of an infinite faculty. But there are certain things which cannot be done (at all) except by an infinite power, such as creating, and other such activities. ... Therefore the soul of

Christ, which, being a creature, is of finite power, may know all things, though not according to every mode of knowing. But it cannot do all things, for this belongs exclusively to the very definition of omnipotence. And it is quite clear, *inter alia*, "among other thing," that it cannot create itself (III, q. 13, a. 1, ad 2).

In these words we have a distinct line of demarcation between power in the soul of Christ and knowledge in the soul of Christ. Are we then to say that his soul (his humanity) has no more power of execution than other human natures? This, of course, theology would not grant. There must be in Christ powers that issue forth from his humanity, as humanity. Let us quote St. Thomas again:

We may consider Christ's soul under a double aspect. In one way according to its own nature and power, be it natural, be it supernatural: in another way as it is the instrument of the Word of God, united personally with him. If therefore we speak of the soul of Christ according to its own nature and power, be it natural, be it supernatural, it had strength to bring about all those effects which belong to his soul; as, for instance, to govern the body, to regulate the human acts and also to illumine, through its own fullness of grace and knowledge, all such rational creatures as are not equal to the perfection of that soul according to the mode which is congenital to the rational creature. But if we speak of the soul of Christ as it is the instrument of the Word of God united with it, from that point of view it had power to bring about such miraculous changes as are conducive to the end of the Incarnation, which end is to restore all things, be it in heaven, be it on earth. But with regard to such changes in creatures as would lead to their extinction (*secundum quod sunt vertibiles in nihil*) they are to be ranked with the creation of things with their production *ex nihilo*. And therefore God who alone can create, alone can bring things back into nothingness (III, q. 13, a. 2, co).

This latter exercise of power St. Thomas, at all times, denies to the soul of Christ. The passage just quoted contains in a few phrases the summary of a far-reaching doctrine of Thomistic theology, the doctrine of instrumental causation. We thus see from the text of St. Thomas that, while denying, as enunciated in the text just quoted, that amplitude to operation which he had granted to intellection, he still concedes to the soul of Christ much in the way of executive. He grants to it the power of illuminating, and this in virtue of its own resources.

A great mystery of spiritual influence in the most real sense is set forth in these words: the soul of Christ is a spirit, the holiest and richest and most active of all spirits, and it operates as a spirit throughout the world of spirits. But great as is his influence, it is not omnipotence. There is also for all external activities, we might say of the physical kind, the instrumental power of the soul of Christ: *Instrumentum Verbi ei uniti*, "an Instrument of the Word united to it." This power we must carefully distinguish from the power attributed to the humanity of Christ, *per communicationem idiomatum*, of which we spoke at the beginning of this chapter.

As a matter of exact theology, let us here say it in passing, that power predicated in virtue of the *communicatio idiomatum* is a point of Catholic faith, whilst the instrumental power here spoken of belongs to speculative theology.

The theory of instrumental power is not restricted, of course, to the Incarnation, but it finds an application in many other branches of Catholic theology, as, for instance, in the doctrine of the Sacraments and in the doctrine of the inspiration of the writers of the books of the Scriptures. In connection with the Incarnation, however, this doctrine receives a higher degree of meaning, as Christ's humanity is called *instrumentum conjunctum Deitatis*, "an instrument united (personally) to the Godhead," while the other instruments are called *instrumenta separata*, "separated instruments," for the simple reason that there is no other instance of a created being being united with God hypostatically.

In a few words, then, confining ourselves here exclusively to the Incarnation, the doctrine is as follows: Christ's humanity, and more directly Christ's soul, is made use of by the Divinity as an instrument of wonderful fitness for bringing about miraculous results in the order of nature and in the order of grace. The circumstance to remember in this matter is the part that Christ's created nature is recognized to bear in bringing about such results. Godhead does not work alone nor does manhood work alone, but the Godhead makes use of the manhood for effects entirely beyond the congenital power of manhood even considered as supernaturally endowed. It is evident that here we have something which is greater than the native powers of Christ's humanity considered in all its enrichments of grace and nature. Again it is something less than the power which belongs to Christ simply in virtue of being the Second Person of the Trinity, as such power is simply and absolutely infinite. Christ's instrumental power—the gift of miracles which he as man possessed in a supreme degree—is something between the two. Of this kind of instrumental power St. Thomas concedes a vast quantity to Christ's soul, though he would say that at no time even instrumental power goes as far in Christ as his human knowledge.

We have said that the doctrine of instrumental power is not directly a matter of faith; but it is a theological conclusion of very great importance. It gives to the humanity of Christ a strength which we instinctively predicate of it. To consider Christ's humanity as being powerful merely because it is hypostatically united to the omnipotent does not seem to satisfy our thirst for reality. Perhaps the Easterns when they fell into the excesses of Monophysitism were groping after a theological notion of that kind. They thought that Christ's humanity should be divinely powerful.

In other portions of the theology of the Incarnation this doctrine is made use of by St. Thomas with great persistence and wonderful sense of the reality of things. He will say, for example, that Christ's Passion and Death as well as his Resurrection act on the spirit world of all ages not only as a moral event but as a physical agent, because Christ's Passion, Death and Resurrection are the *instrumenta conjuncta* of the Godhead for the raising up of the spirit world.

10

THE MORTALITY OF CHRIST

ITHERTO WE HAVE FOLLOWED CATHOLIC THEOLOGY in stating the principles and pursuing to the last consequences all that is contained in those principles concerning the fullness of Christ's personality and life. We come now to that portion of Christology which is absolutely indispensable to the mystery of Christ and which may be considered as the opposite of that fullness, the emptying out, the infirmity, the poverty of Christ. Moderns call this the "kenotic" aspect of the Incarnation, from Greek terms which signify "emptying out," as if we had to imagine that Christ was made empty of certain perfections which he might have possessed. But for this "emptying out," be it voluntary or be it unavoidable, the older phrase, the phrase of Catholic theology is more accurate. It puts the matter thus: *Utrum Filius Dei in humana natura assumere debuerit cor ports defectus*: "Whether Christ in the Incarnation took upon himself imperfections of soul and body" (III, q. 14, a. 1). The word defectus here used does not mean "defect" in the sense of warping, of anything abnormal, but merely an absence of certain qualities, something negative, a deprivation or imperfection.

That Christ appeared with such imperfection in his human nature is part of Christian faith. He could suffer in his bodily frame, he
could die, he could with all truthfulness be sad in his soul even unto
death. To admit this belongs to the very heart of the mystery of our
Redemption in Christ; to deny it is to deny the work of our salvation. It is necessary, of course, in order to understand this doctrine of
Christ's mortality to take for granted much else that belongs to the
general theology of man's relations with God. We must assume that
suffering and death entered this world through sin, that they are the
penalty of sin, that through them man may give satisfaction for sin
committed, that Christ shared those human conditions out of love
and that by taking upon himself these universal consequences of sin
he gave infinite satisfaction for sin, as he is an infinite Person. Moreover, by sharing our mortality he completely altered man's outlook;
no longer could suffering and death be considered to be absolute evils
when the Son of God had consented to bear them in his own body.
Unless we be prepared to accept these traditional views concerning
the nature of human suffering and human death, it would be futile to
proceed with the theology of the Incarnation.

The mortality of Christ is irrevocably identified with those traditional views of the Christian faith concerning evil. St. Thomas fre-
quently repeats a principle which must be our guide also in this matter of Christ's infirmities. Christ took upon himself such infirmities
(*defectus*) as were conducive to that end of the Incarnation which is
called the Redemption, the satisfaction for sin. If there is a doubt
whether any particular form of infirmity was in Christ, the only question to ask is this: would that particular infirmity be conducive to the
end of the Redemption, to the healing of sins? In the light of such
a principle St. Thomas exercises a most laudable moderation; he is

reluctant to multiply the infirmities of Christ; if anything he does the contrary. So from the very outset he makes it evident that no gain could come to us through any diminution in Christ's supernatural and truly spiritual riches, in his grace, in his knowledge, in his innocence. Satisfaction for sin, he says, has a twofold element: the material element of physical suffering and death, and the immaterial element of the charity that is behind it. Now it would be a diminution of Christ's charity if there were in his soul less light, less perfection, less sanctity. And such an emptying out, far from helping us, would defeat the end of the Incarnation. Then there is another principle of which St. Thomas never tires, that Christ's mortality is accepted by him, not absolutely for its own sake, as are his positive qualities, but *dispensative* for the sake of an end to be attained, provisionally, with a wise adjustment between means and ends. Not every kind of suffering, not every sort of mortality is to be predicated of Christ; but such only as belong to the human nature considered in its universality since the Fall.

There is a necessary element of externality in the causes that bring about suffering and death in Christ. He had not in himself the seed of death as other men have. He could not have died of old age, but he could be killed by men. The causes of his sadness, also, were external to himself. He is essentially the Victim, the *Agnus Dei*, "Lamb of God," that is immolated. For this reason St. Thomas is very insistent that we should say that in the Incarnation Christ took upon himself infirmities, but "did not contract them": *non contraxit*. The word *contrahere* implies an hereditary taint, a subjection to a law of sin, to a curse, because we belong to the same race. Such was not Christ's case. Even when he became Man he was not in any way bound to take upon himself the conditions of mortality, for mortality belongs to man only in the hypothesis of sin, and so with the other defects.

Still we have to admit that when once it had been determined that Christ should be born mortal and infirm, in the restricted sense of a voluntary dispensation, the consequences of that initial resolve on the part of the Son of God to appear in the form of a slave—to use St. Paul's expression—followed naturally and inevitably. It may be said that it was really a miracle that the God Incarnate should appear in mortality, as power and glory and immortality belong to him by every right and even by a physical law; but that, granted this state, the daily and experimental realization of the state of mortality were not miraculous phenomena. St. Thomas more than once uses the expression that the glories which were in the superior regions of Christ's human nature were kept from overflowing into certain other regions of his nature as they might have done, lest the end of the Incarnation—satisfaction for sin—should not be attained. It is easy, therefore, to see that with all our faith in Christ's mortality we must banish from him every vestige of sin and every kind of ignorance, as sin and ignorance would evidently not be helpful towards the end of the Incarnation.

Nor was there in him the *fomes peccati*, "the internal temptation to sin," as his flesh was formed, not by man but by the Holy Ghost in the womb of the Virgin. Though it may be said in a relative sense that sin and temptation could be the occasion of virtue, because repentance for sin is laudable and vanquished temptation is praiseworthy, still it was not necessary for Christ to be virtuous through such occasions. He showed his detestation of sin by dying for its satisfaction as an innocent victim, and he showed supreme virtue by having every fiber of his being under the influence of perfect sanctity.

We admit in Christ the existence of what is called passion. In that state of mortality in which he was born he could suffer in his soul as other men are said to suffer in their souls, through sadness, through fear, through pain. He could have wonder and anger in his soul. But all these emotions are called by St. Thomas more truly "propassions." By this difference of expression the great Doctor means something which it is also necessary for us to remember: whatever emotions were in Christ's soul they could never be real disturbances in it. As an interesting instance of the realism of our theology concerning the Person of Christ we may mention the doctrine of St. Thomas that in our Lord there was true *admiratio*, "wonderment." He was astonished, he marveled, he was surprised. This, of course, is only a conclusion of what we said concerning the human knowledge of Christ's soul. *Admiratio* could not be in him in virtue of his divine vision nor in virtue of his infused angelic knowledge, as such modes of knowing are complete from the beginning and nothing new is shown to the mind because the understanding is not progressive. But as, according to the best theologians, there is also in Christ acquired and experimental knowledge coming from his powers of human observation, he could truly learn new things every day in that sphere of his being, and accordingly he could be struck with wonder as other men are.

All this is only an enlargement of the central principle of theology that Christ was at the same time both *comprehensor* and *viator*. In the exact language of St. Thomas:

> Christ for this reason was at the same time *comprehensor*, because he had that blessedness which belongs to the soul, and he was also a *viator* because he was moving towards blessedness in such things as were wanting to his blessedness (III, q. 15, a. 10).

The things that were wanting were, again, such as came from that state of soul which enabled him to be subject to passion and that state of body which made suffering and death possible.

It is evident from the preceding considerations which are so paramount in orthodox Christology, that what we might call the interior life of Christ—to use a modern phrase—is indeed a great mystery, a state of experience completely unknown to us except in some of its minor elements. The presence of the Beatific Vision, with its concomitant beatific fruition, places the psychology of the mortal Christ in an entirely singular category of life. On the other hand nothing could be more dangerous than to refuse to accept in their literalness such words as St. Matthew's rendering of Christ's agony of soul, "My soul is sorrowful even unto death. Stay you here and watch with me" (Matt 26:38).

For our guidance and for our edification it is enough that we should know that Christ's soul was sorrowful unto death, though it be not possible for us to understand how such sorrow could be in One to whom all things were clear in the blessed light of God. It is not useless to reiterate the fact that the best kind of theology proceeds with great prudence in this matter of describing the infirmities of Christ. We are on less certain ground here than we are in the matter of Christ's supernatural enrichments and endowments. These latter are the immediate and permanent consequences of the hypostatic union, while the former are essentially means to an end, of a transient and provisional nature.

11

The Language of the Incarnation

I T MUST BE EVIDENT TO EVERYONE THAT NOTHING COULD be more important than the language in which we express all that concerns Christ. The Catholic Church has exercised special watchfulness over the way in which her children speak of the Son of God. As Christ is one Person in two natures, and as one of the two natures is not divine or infinite while the other is divine and infinite, it is obvious that there are many pitfalls for human language in the attempt to speak of the Son of God. The fundamental principle to guide us in finding out the correctness or the inaccuracy or even falseness of any special phrase in Christology is this, that Christ is essentially and always and above all things a divine Person. He is a human nature only partially, in the sense that human nature is on the whole a comparatively small portion of his being, and that in no sense an independent portion. So whatever we say of Christ is to be said of him without any qualification, absolutely, directly, without any explanation. Whatever takes place in Christ, be it in his human nature, be it in his divine nature, is predicated of him as of the Son of God without any reservation. This Person, Christ, the Son of God, is eternal, is infinite, is all-holy, is omnipotent, is invisible. But this Person, Christ, is with equal truthfulness of expression, born in time, born of a Virgin; he lived on earth, he was made visible, he suffered on the Cross and he died thereon, he rose again on the third day. In other words, whatever is found in the human nature as well as in the divine nature is to be predicated directly of the Person Christ, of the second Person of the Trinity, because the second Person of the Trinity is the *suppositum*, the "personality" of both natures indistinctively.

In older theological language this is called the *communicatio idiomatum*, the "interchange of properties." Everything that belongs to the human nature is predicated of the divine Person, and whatever belongs to the divine nature is, of course, also predicated of the divine Person. We do not say that what belongs to the human nature is predicated of the divine nature and vice versa. It is the Person that is the *tertium quid*, "third thing," in which this exchange takes place. When, for instance, we use phrases like this, that the immortal is also mortal, we mean that one and the same Person at one and the same time has mortality and immortality; that one and the same Person is eternal and yet was born and died in time. We do not assert that an immortal nature has become a mortal nature or vice versa, but that an immortal Person has assumed a nature which could die.

This *tertium quid* in which natures meet, according to an expression of St. Thomas already quoted, is indispensable to all our knowledge and all our language in this matter of the Incarnation. If it is asked how one and the same Person could be thus the subject of entirely opposite conditions such as mortality and immortality, the answer given rests on a qualification, a qualification not necessary, as already said, when we speak of the doings of the Person itself. We say, then, that a divine Person is mortal in his human nature and immortal in his divine nature. The whole power of the Incarnation, its redemptive power, its meritoriousness, rests on this, the objective reality of the *communicatio idiomatum*, namely, that it should be true in all languages that God died on the Cross; though he died in his human nature, still the death was the death of the Son of God. This is the full mystery of the Hypostatic Union, the union *in persona* as defined by the Council of Ephesus. To say that anyone but God died on the Cross is, of course, heresy. This is also the reason why Mary is truly the Mother of God, because the One born of her is God not man.

Even if we say that the birth at Bethlehem was according to Christ's manhood, still the One who came forth from the Virgin's womb was God as fully as the One who is engendered by the Father from all eternity. If anyone, for instance, should say that Christ's humanity died on the Cross, his statement would be dangerously near to heresy, because the subject of the phrase is not a person but a nature which is not independent. "God died on the Cross" would be the full orthodox expression, and if we seek to qualify it we may add that he died in his humanity, though such qualification in no wise diminishes the meaning of the death of the Son of God; morally, meritoriously, with all the implications of ethical responsibility, it is simply God that died. Whether it be in his humanity or divinity is irrelevant to the spiritual and juridical aspect of the case.

There are three phrases which are current in Christian language and which are equally orthodox:

Deus est homo: "God is man."

Homo est Deus: "Man is God."

Deus factus est homo: "God was made man."

A fourth phrase, *Homo factus est Deus*, "Man was made God," is open to many objections and should not be employed. The third phrase, *Deus factus est homo* is, of course, the oldest and the best known. It is the same as the *Verbum caro factum est*, "the Word was made flesh," of the Gospel of St. John (John 1:14). With all we have said concerning the role of person in the mystery of the Incarnation we ought to be ready to see the complete appropriateness of such a mode of speech. It only means that a divine Person, in time, took unto himself a human nature. Divine personality is predicated of human nature. As such a condition of things did not exist from all eternity, but happened in time, the *factus est*, "was made," is, of course, most appropriate. God became something which he was not before—man.

For the same reasons the expression "God is man" is grammatically accurate, and theologically orthodox. A divine Person is man because that manhood stands *in rerum natura* "in the nature of things," in virtue of that divine Person. It is what it is entirely on account of that Person. The opposite mode of putting it, that "Man is God," is literal and accurate. That singular human nature is the nature of a divine Person:

> The divine Person is the hypostasis of that human nature. *Dicimus (Personam Filii Dei) esse hypostasim humanae naturae* (III, q. 16, a. 2).

That human nature cannot call itself its own, it entirely belongs to the second Person of the Trinity.

The reason why we object to the phrase "Man was made God" is obvious: such a phrase would suppose that one who already existed as man became God at a given moment of time, which would imply a personal and independent existence of that man. So there is no counterpart to the phrase *Deus factus est homo*. A divine Person existed and assumed unto himself a human nature, but there existed no human nature that could be united to a divine Person, for if it had existed before the union it would have been a person, which is against the central idea of the Hypostatic Union.

12

WILL POWER IN THE GOD INCARNATE

Thus far we have seen how oneness of Person in Christ means the presence in him of created gifts and qualities which are the necessary consequences of that oneness of Person in the duality of natures. Grace and knowledge in Christ's human nature are the concomitant elements of the oneness of the divine Person. When we come to the volitive side in Christ's Person, the duality and the difference between the human and the divine in him is more accentuated, because there is, as we shall see, a possibility of at least apparent opposition between the divine and the human in this matter of Christ's will-power. Of all the heresies and errors directly concerning the Person of Jesus Christ, aberrations with regard to this point have lasted longest and have been latest condemned. Monothelitism is a heresy about the will of Christ. It disturbed the Church, even the Western Church, right down to the Middle Ages, and through its manifold uncertainties compromised even a Pope in the person of Honorius I. Monothelitism was condemned in the Sixth General Council. It maintains, as the Greek root of the word implies, that in Christ there is only one will a divine will of course. It is, as everyone can see, a limited sort of monophysitism, restricting the oneness of nature in Christ to the will-power only, whereas Eutyches had made that oneness co-extensive with Christ's human nature, teaching that the whole of Christ's human nature was absorbed by the divine nature.

The origins of Monothelitism seem to have been ascetical rather than dogmatical. Ascetics have always held up the will as a dangerous element. To be one with God's will has ever been considered as the ascetical perfection. Difference of will between the divine and the human, to the eye of the ascetic, is tantamount to sin. It is not surprising, then, that Monophysitism should in a way be resuscitated in the shape of Monothelitism, which considers Christ's human will to have been absorbed by God's will. Traditional faith, however, was not to be diverted from its wonderful balance by the exaggerations of Eastern asceticism; it maintains that will as much as intellect belongs to the completeness of the human nature, as an essential constituent thereof. If Christ, in his human nature, were devoid of will he would not be man in the true sense and the Incarnation would be jeopardized. Moreover, the absence of the power of will in Christ's humanity would mean absence of the power of merit, and thus the whole economy of grace, which is based on the merits of Christ, would collapse.

So our scholastic theology has no difficulty in building up a truly wonderful doctrine concerning the will-power of Christ, its multiplicity of nature, its liberty of action, its conformity with the Will of the Father and also its possible differences. The classification of will-power in Christ is different from the classification of the various kinds of knowledge in Christ. There is in Christ the divine will that is to say, the will of the divine nature, and there is also the human will. There is nothing in this matter of will corresponding to that angelic kind of knowledge which we attributed to Christ's intellect in a former chapter. Christ's human will is entirely human, exclusively human; it follows all the laws of the human will excepting, of course, all possibility of failure or sin. So, like every human will it is twofold: it is rational and it is sensitive.

This distinction is profound and far-reaching; besides the rational will, which is connected with the intellect, there is in man the will of the *appetitus*, "the lower will." Technically we call it the will of sensuality, but we give to this term its philosophical meaning, which stands for the whole sphere of those appetitive instincts in man which come from the play of all the senses. This appetitive will is given a very high place in man's life by our best scholastics, and they say that it is rational by participation, that is to say, in man the appetite of the senses has a certain nobility which comes of proximity to that faculty which is entirely rational and intellectual. Now, the whole of Catholic theology is emphatic in attributing to Christ this twofold will-power, without any inhibition. Thus *voluntas sensualis*, "sensual will," is boldly predicated of him as an integral part of his wonderful personality. It had its full play under the higher will which rests in the intellect directly. This higher will the rational will is divided again by the Catholic philosopher into *voluntas rationis*, "will of reason," and *voluntas naturae*, "will of nature," but this distinction is not exclusive to man, it belongs to all intellectual beings. By the aforesaid distinction of will of the intellectual kind certain necessities are implied: it must, by the very laws of its nature, embrace goodness, either real or apparent. It cannot, for instance, run away from infinite goodness if that infinite goodness be clearly shown to it. The *voluntas rationis*, on the other hand, is based on choice and election, it is concerned with the finite good. The will can accept it or reject it after deliberation. It goes without saying that the human will of Christ, like all other created will is thus constituted.

Coming now to that oneness of will which is said to exist between God and man in all true sanctity, we have to make the far-reaching distinction, so often neglected, between will as an object and will as a faculty. Two distinct wills may have one object, but two distinct wills can never be one faculty. It is this identity of object which is the consummation of sanctity, i.e. that the created will should embrace the object which the increated will embraces, whatever that object may be. It is in that sense that God's will becomes our will that we ask from God that his will be done. But it is certainly remarkable that St. Thomas should have allowed a kind of diversity between Christ's human will and God's will in this very matter of the object. He states that Christ's lower will which as we have said, is a great power, did not embrace the object which God's will put before it, i.e. suffering and death. It shrank from it. It was only the higher will in him, the will of election, that accepted those commands of the Father; the lower will according to St. Thomas, could not naturally be one with such objects. All that was necessary for Christ's perfection was that the final election of the will should be entirely in conformity with the Father. The words of Christ in his agony are the best authority for establishing the soundness of Catholic theology on his varied will-power: "Father, if thou wilt, remove this chalice from me, but yet not my will but thine be done" (Luke 22:42).

We cannot admit any contrariety between the Father and the Incarnate Son in this matter of the will but we may certainly speak of differences. St. Thomas gives this principle which is far-reaching and important in other provinces of Catholic theology:

There is contrariety of will then only when the same kind of will is opposed to the same kind of object (III, q. 18 a. 6).

Say that the rational will in two persons be in opposition concerning one and the same measure to be adopted or plan to be followed. St. Thomas gives us a broad example, the case of a prince and a private person. The prince orders a man to be put to death for a crime. It would be perfectly legitimate for the father of the condemned man to feel distress and even opposition to the prince's commands. But if this opposition meant a determination to set at naught the prince's measure for the defense of the public good, there would be real contrariety of will between the subject and the ruler. Moreover, there is no irregularity or contrariety of wills if the lower will shrinks from a task as long as the higher will overrules such a sentiment.

It is truly remarkable to what an extent St. Thomas allows full play to the human will of Christ under the will of the Godhead. This comes from the state of possibility in Christ; in fact, it is part of that state of possibility that his lower will should shrink from pain and death. Herein Christ differs from the elect in heaven from the point of view of will. The state of blessedness has no tasks or commands which in any way could be a burden to the elect. In that state those differences of will which we admit in the Incarnate Son of God while here on earth do not exist because the state is so different.

The freedom of the human will of Christ is taken for granted because Christ had to merit eternal life for man and all merit presupposes freedom of will. There is of course in Christ absolute impeccability. He could not sin, he could not in any way disobey a command laid on him by the Father. But this impeccability is not against the exercise of free-will. The elect in heaven possess complete impeccability and yet they are free in their will. So Christ received the command of the Father to lay down his life with complete freedom of choice, as the elect in heaven carry out with entire freedom any of God's behests. When Gabriel received the command to journey to Nazareth to the Virgin Mary, he obeyed freely though we all know that disobedience was impossible to him. When Christ received the command to die on the Cross he also obeyed freely, though in his case, too, disobedience was impossible.

13

CHRIST'S OPERATIONS

ALTHOUGH IT HAS BEEN MADE CLEAR THAT ALL REALITY in the Person of Christ is twofold, human and divine—with the exception of the actual personal *esse* which in him is emphatically and essentially one—special attention has still to be paid to the workings, the operations of the God-Man, and those workings we have to consider in their twofold acceptations, internal and external. There is in this matter of Christ's operations a particular aspect which does not occur in those realities in his Person which are mere qualities. A work, an act, seems to be more particularly attributed to a person, and as in Christ there is only one Person, it would seem that all these workings are as one. It is, however, evident from the outset that both natures in Christ, the human and the divine, have their special workings. The human will loves and carries out its intention in external activities; the divine will loves and carries out its own purposes. After all that has been said no concerning the preservation of the human nature in its entirety in Hypostatic Union it is not necessary further to elaborate this truth.

There are in Christ the two operations, or, if we prefer so to express it, the two sets of operations, the human and divine. But this duality cannot be left without a profound modification. What we might call the responsibility, the imputability of the operations must be put down entirely to the one Person. It is the Son of God who does everything we know of him. He heals the sick, he walks on the waters, he eats and he drinks, he loves, and he rebukes his enemies. All these acts are to be attributed to the Person. Though we may say that many of his works are done in his human nature, still they are done by himself, by the one indivisible Person, the Son of God. He has the full merit of those acts, their full responsibility: this is a necessary consequence of the oneness of Person in him. The divine nature in Christ has the human so much in its grasp that there is no kind of operation in him, I mean in his human nature, which is not completely under the control of his divinity.

In this matter St. Thomas makes an observation which shows that to his mind the human psychology of Christ stood in a category apart. He wants to show that in our Lord all the movements of his human nature were harmonious and converging towards the one center of his personality, the divine will.

> In the man Jesus Christ there was no movement in the sense-part of his being which was not ordered by reason. For even his natural and corporal operations were under the control of his will; for it was part of his will that his flesh should do and suffer what belongs to the flesh. ... And therefore oneness of operation in Christ (in his human nature) is much greater than in any other man (III, q. 19, a, 2).

Here we may describe Christ's human workings as being the instruments of his divinity. This metaphor, however, whilst saving the duality of the operations, expresses also the oneness of responsibility. The term "theandric" has been applied to the operations of Christ, as being works which are at the same time both of God and of man.

In this connection we may further speak of Christ's power of merit. To begin with, could he merit for himself? The answer of St. Thomas is profound. He says that there are certain created gifts which it is more glorious to possess through merit, whilst there are other gifts which it is more glorious to possess, not through merit but through a kind of birthright. To possess grace, knowledge, Beatific Vision, even Hypostatic Union through heredity, so to speak, is better than to possess them through merit. But to merit through charity the glory of the body, the Ascension into heaven, the exaltation in the eyes of all creation is more glorious than to have such privileges without merit, for it shows what charity can do. Therefore we grant that Christ merited these latter privileges for himself.

Of course we only say this in the supposition that, through a special dispensation, Christ appeared amongst men *in forma servi*, "in the form of a servant" (Phil 2:7), without being thus endowed actually. The Father left the Son through the death on the Cross to merit for himself to be raised above all names. That Christ merited for men eternal life is, of course, the very essence of the Christian dogma of man's salvation. He could merit for man because he was established from the very beginning as the mystical head of mankind. Man is not really a separate entity from Christ; man is part of his mystical body. It would not be logical to say that Christ merited only for those who are actually part of his mystical body through Baptism. Christ truly merited for men the first grace of justification, that very privilege of being incorporated into him, because through what he did and suffered he merited from the Father to be the mystical head of mankind;

therefore when any man through the grace of God is incorporated in God his first incorporation is a result of Christ's merits: "This very thing is part of Christ's grace that it is granted to man to be first regenerated," *Hoc ipsum est gratiae, quod homini conceditur regenerari in Christo* (III, q. 19, a. 4, ad 3).

14

CHRIST'S SUBJECTION TO THE FATHER AND CHRIST'S PRIESTHOOD

W E COME NOW TO A PORTION OF CATHOLIC CHRISTOLOGY which may be described as Christ's relationship to the Father. We mean, of course, by this expression "to the Father" the first Person of the Trinity, but not in an exclusive sense. Christ is the Son of the Father in an exclusive sense because the first Person of the Trinity begot the second Person from all eternity. But when we speak of other relationships, such as Christ's subjection to the Father, Christ's predestination by the Father, Christ's Priesthood, the term Father really stands for the whole Godhead, because all the aforesaid relationships are founded in Christ's humanity and therefore they are directed to the whole Trinity, to the second Person as much as to the first Person. In this sense we can say with St. Thomas that Christ was subject, not only to the Father, but also to himself, for this subjection is essentially in the human nature:

> We may say that according to that nature which he has in common
> with the Father, (Christ) with the Father likewise is supreme, is

the Lord. But according to the other nature in which he resembles us Christ is an inferior, he can serve. And in this sense St. Augustine could say that Christ is inferior to himself (III, q. 20, a. 2).

In that sense the prayer of Christ as well as the sacrifice of Christ was addressed to the second Person as well as to the first, because the prayer and the sacrifice were done in his human nature. Christ likewise can be said to have been predestinated by God to be the Son of God:

Predestination is to be attributed to Christ by the reason of his human nature alone, for the human nature was not always united to the Word, and it was through divine grace that the privilege was granted that it should be united to the Son of God in Person, and therefore solely by reason of human nature can it be said that predestination is predicated of Christ (III, q. 24, a. 2).

All the same it would be wrong to say that it was human nature that was predestined, though Christ was predestined solely on account of human nature:

It has to be concluded therefore that predestination must be attributed to the Person of Christ not indeed on account of itself or as it subsists in the divine nature, but as it subsists in the human nature (III, q. 24, a. 1, ad 2).

The most sacred relationship of Christ with the Father (in the sense in which we here define that relationship) is Christ's Priesthood. Whatever the Scriptures say of priesthood is to be attributed to Christ, minus the imperfections of the priesthood. We know Christ to be a Priest because, firstly, we have the direct utterances of the Scriptures giving him the name of Priest:

We have a great high priest that hath passed into the heavens, Jesus the Son of God. *Habemus Pontificem qui penetravit coelos, Jesum Filium Dei* (Heb 4:14).

Secondly, Christ is repeatedly said to fulfill such functions as constitute priesthood. Above all, Christ has reconciled the human race to God; now reconciliation is the supreme ministry of the priesthood:

In him, it hath well pleased the Father that all fullness should dwell. In ipso complacuit omnem plenitudinem inhabitare et per eum reconciliare omnia (Col. 1:19).

It is evident that in this matter of Christ's priesthood we are using concepts and terms which come from the revealed and institutional religion of the Jews. The mission of the Son of God is essentially a work for the glory of God and for the spiritual and eternal advantage of men. Such work has been described in the Old Testament as "priesthood"—*sacerdotium*. Christ did such work in the highest possible degree; therefore the whole traditional phraseology concerning priesthood is applicable to him. In the same sense Christ is also a victim because he fulfills spiritual functions of such a nature as can only be carried out by the victim of a sacrifice. What the powers of a sacrificial victim are we know only from revealed religion: the victim of a sacrifice keeps man united with God; the victim of a sacrifice leads man to the possession of God in glory. Such functions are attributed to the sacrificial victim through a divine institution.

Now, as Christ fulfilled all those functions eminently, he is rightly called a victim, besides being the priest. These are the reasons which St. Thomas uses in order to establish the traditional truth that Christ was a victim. St. Thomas does not directly discuss the mode in which he was a victim; he takes it for granted, at least in the case of Christ, that he was a victim, a *hostia*, through death. There is, however, an apparently grave objection against the assertion that Christ is a victim through death, as his death was an act of violence on the part of the men who put him to death. To this St. Thomas gives the answer which is at the root of Christ's whole position as sacrifice:

> Christ's death may be related to a twofold will firstly to the will of those who killed him, and from that point of view Christ's death has not the nature of a victim. ... Secondly, Christ's death (*occisio*) may be related to the will of him to suffer who offered himself freely to the Passion. And from that point of view Christ's death has the nature of a victim (III, q. 22, a. 2, ad 1).

St. Thomas considers the priesthood of Christ to be coextensive with his work of redemption; in fact, to be the same office as the office of redemption. It merits all the graces which are necessary for man's salvation and for the purification of sin, and it satisfies fully unto God's justice for all the sins of man. So St. Thomas concludes, "Christ's priesthood is not something less than Christ's redemption," *Unde patet quod Christi Sacerdotium habet plenam vim expiandi peccata* (III, q. 22, a. 3).

The answer of St. Thomas to the first objection in the third article of the Twenty-second Question is to be noted. The objector says that Christ's Priesthood could not be an expiation of sin because God alone can destroy sin. Now, "Christ was Priest, not in his divine nature but in his human nature," *Christus non est Sacerdos secundum quod Deus sed secundum quod homo* (III, q. 22, a. 5, ob 3); therefore Christ's Priesthood could not expiate sin. The answer is: Although Christ was not Priest according to his divine nature, but according to his human nature, still one and the same Person was Priest and God. This expiation of sin by Christ's priesthood was complete when he offered himself as sacrifice at his death.

> The sacrifice which is offered up daily by the Church is not a different sacrifice from the one which Christ offered up, but it is its memory. *Sacrificium autem quod quotidie in Ecclesia offeretur, non est aliud a sacrificio quod ipse Christus obtulit, sed ejus commemoratio* (III, q. 22, a. 3, ad 2).

It is evidently a consequence to be deduced from the doctrine of Hypostatic Union that Christ could not be said to have offered up a sacrifice for himself for he is not in a state to be benefited by any such sacrifice. Though it may be said that the glorification of his body followed upon his sacrifice, yet that cannot be described as a result of the sacrifice as man's salvation is a result of that sacrifice. Christ's glorification is the fruit of that great charity which he showed in offering up the sacrifice. Says St. Thomas:

Christ obtained through his Passion the glory of the Resurrection, not through the power of the sacrifice (*non quasi ex vi sacrificii*) which is offered up by way of satisfaction, but through that devotedness which made him suffer his Passion with meekness according to charity (III, q. 22, a. 4, ad 2).

Christ, again, is "a Priest forever," *Sacerdos in aeternum*, not in the sense that he offers up a sacrifice forever in heaven, but in the sense of his consummating a sacrifice by bringing about that end which is the end of all sacrifice, the union of man with God. According to St. Thomas the office of a priest is double: *Primo quidem ipsa oblatio sacrificii, secundo ipsa sacrificii consumatio*, "First indeed is the offering of the sacrifice itself; second is the consummation of that sacrifice" (III,

q. 22, a. 5). This consummation is truly part of the priesthood, and the Lamb is said to lead the elect to God in glory. This is the traditional meaning of the heavenly sacrifice, not an *oblatio sacrificii*, "offering of the sacrifice," in heaven but a *consumatio sacrificii*, "consummation of the sacrifice."

15

THE CULT OF CHRIST

HONOR IS GIVEN DIRECTLY TO A PERSON AND THEREFORE where there is one person there is also one honor; where there is a multiplicity of persons there is also multiplicity of honors. But in the same person there may be a variety of reasons which command honor; one and the same person may be honored for the nobility of his birth and for the excellency of his mental qualities, his science and wisdom; still the honor paid will be directed, not to the various excellencies of the person but to the person himself. As Christ is a divine Person the honor to be paid to him is the same which is paid to God, and therefore whatever constitutes the Person of Christ is worthy of divine honor. So we have to conclude that the same honor, in other words, the same adoration, is to be given to Christ's humanity which is bestowed upon Christ's divinity, simply for the reason that Christ's humanity is part of a divine Person.

If Nestorianism were true, then two different honors would be paid to Christ, different in kind: adoration would be addressed to the divinity and some other kind of worship to the humanity. But with the Catholic doctrine of oneness of Person it is evident that divine honors have to be paid to Christ's humanity. The honor to be paid to Christ's Person is essentially *latria*, i.e. a worship based on the incommunicable property of God that he is the origin and end of all things. That Christ's humanity should receive such honor is simply a conclusion from the oneness of Person in the Hypostatic Union. Though Christ's humanity in itself is not the origin and end of all things, still it is part of the Person of One who is the origin and end of all beings.

Medieval theologians, with St. Thomas, speak of another kind of honor: *dulia*. *Latria*, of which we have spoken, is always and everywhere *adoratio*, "adoration," in the quite exclusive sense in which modern thought uses the word. *Dulia* may be *adoratio* but is not necessarily so. It is honor paid for excellencies, which may be in God and may be in the creature, analogically, of course. That first property of God, that he is the beginning and end of all things, is not to be found in the creature, even analogically; but other perfections may be ascribed analogically to the creature.

The medieval theologian, then, contended that the honor we pay to God for such of his perfections as are communicable to creatures analogically, is to be called *dulia*. It is a worship which creatures also may receive for the simple reason that they can share in God's perfections. According to medieval theology, then, it is to be gathered from the subject to whom worship is paid whether adoration in the technical sense or some inferior mode of worship is intended. In the case of God, *dulia* is adoration pure and simple; in fact, it is then only to be distinguished logically from *latria*. In the case of creatures, *dulia* has degrees as the excellencies of the creatures also vary. In strict Thomist theology, *dulia* is the name for any honor we pay to God or creature. The Mother of God, being the most excellent of all creatures and being unique on account of her Motherhood, is worshipped with *hyperdulia*, which word only means *dulia* of a higher grade. *Dulia* has a universality of meaning which is to be borne in mind as its special characteristic.

The question then arises whether Christ, besides receiving *latria*, ought also to receive *dulia*. That he receives the kind of *dulia* which is given to God and which it has been said is only logically to be distinguished from *latria*, is evident from the principles of oneness of personality. But is Christ's Person to be worshipped with *dulia* on account of his participated perfections, on account of the glories and graces of his humanity? The answer is in the affirmative. As there are obviously created perfections in Christ's Person, and as every created perfection may be an object of *dulia*, we cannot deny to Christ the worship of *dulia*. In the words of Cajetan, on account of Christ's divinity of Person he receives the worship of *latria* and on account of his humanity the divine Person of Christ receives also the worship of *dulia*. Here, of course, we oppose *dulia* to *latria* as being based on created perfections or analogical resemblance with God.

It may further be asked what is the specific degree of that *dulia* which is founded on Christ's created perfections. St. Thomas seems to call it *hyperdulia*, which term settles nothing. Is this *dulia*, as addressed to Christ's Person, adoration or not? Or, more explicitly, does this *dulia* worship excellency which is in some way infinite? We may certainly admit that those created excellencies of Christ's personality are infinite in some way though not in every way; therefore we may hold that in the case of the Person of Christ *dulia* worships those things that are infinite. Whether this may be called adoration or not we need not settle.

Cajetan again makes the remark that, to avoid confusion of mind in her children, the Church has not pressed the point of this worship of *dulia* in the Person of Christ. The overpowering worship of *latria* is, of course, infinitely more necessary in the Church's life and with *latria* she worships everything in Christ, his body and his blood, his heart and his head, his acts and his thoughts.

Worship of all degrees, be it *latria*, be it *dulia*, is twofold: it is either absolute or relative. The absolute worship goes direct to the person honored, the relative worship also goes to the person but through the representation of the person, such as a statue or a painted image. In relative worship we adopt all the language which belongs to the absolute because in reality the homage is one and the same. So we say that we adore the image of Christ: we adore his Cross because he is the crucified; we worship the image of the Mother of God and of the Saints with the same *dulia* which belongs to the Mother of God and the Saints themselves.

From this it follows that it would be unwise to attribute to the images of Christ and of the Saints any other worship than the complete *latria* or *dulia* according to each case, for the whole reason of that cult is the relationship of the representation with its prototype. No other cult may be paid to images. Therefore unless we admit the complete *dulia* or *latria* there is no reason for admitting any other degree of worship.

There are, however, objects which the Church blesses and consecrates, and among these there are also representations of Christ and the Saints. From that point of view they belong to the sacramentals, they are not considered in their relative value as representations of something higher. They are to be honored with a cult which has nothing in common with the cult of the representative objects as such; they are to be revered as holy things consecrated by the Church.

16

THE PASSION AND THE DEATH OF CHRIST

IT IS TO BE LAID DOWN AS A FIRST PRINCIPLE IN THE MATTER of Christ's Passion that he was put to death, effectively, not by himself but by men. Men killed him because what they did to him was sufficient to bring about death. There is, however, that other most important aspect in Christ's Passion, that this death was free and voluntary, and that it had redeeming power on that very account. How it was voluntary St. Thomas explains thus:

> In another way something is the cause of an event indirectly because one does not prevent when one could prevent. ... In this sense Christ was the cause of his Passion and his death. This he could do in the first place by checking his enemies so that they would be either unwilling or powerless to kill him; secondly, because his spirit had it in its power to preserve the nature of his flesh so that it could not be overcome by any kind of hurt inflicted on it. Such power the soul of Christ possessed because it was united in Person to the Word of God (III, q. 47, a. 1).

Again St. Thomas sums up the history of Christ's Passion from the point of view of Christ's liberty in it in these words:

> As through his will his bodily nature was kept in its vigor to the very end, thus also, when he willed it, that nature succumbed to the hurt which was inflicted on it (III, q. 47, a. 1, ad 2).

Once more St. Thomas says:

> Christ at the same time suffered such violence that he should die of it, and yet he died freely, voluntarily, because violence was done to his body, which violence, however, only did as much harm to his body as he allowed (III, q. 47, a. 1, ad 3).

In the same sense we have to understand the expressions in the Scriptures, that the Father gave up his Son unto his Passion:

> He spared not even his own Son, but delivered him up for us all. *Proprio Filio non pepercit Deus sed pro nobis omnibus tradidit illum* (Rom 8:32).

From all eternity God preordained the Passion of Christ as the remedy of sin; then he gave to Christ the inspiration of laying down his life, and thirdly he allowed Christ to fall into the hands of his enemies. Thus we must understand Christ's exclamation on the Cross: *Deus meus, Deus meus, ut quid dereliquisti me?* "My God, my God, why hast Thou forsaken me?" (Matt 27:46):

> The Father delivered up Christ and Christ himself did so out of charity and therefore they are praised; Judas delivered Christ from avarice, the Jews from envy, Pilate from human fear because he feared Caesar, and therefore they are blamed (III, q. 47. a. 3, ad 3).

With this principle of Christ's perfect freedom in laying down his life it is easy to understand how, on the Cross, he fulfilled the highest spiritual functions, all of which presuppose freedom. Christ on the Cross is satisfaction, Christ on the Cross is redemption. It is in these ways he brought about our salvation. Whether these modes enumerated by St. Thomas are one and the same thing viewed from these different aspects or are really different modes, need not be decided. It is certain that Christ on the Cross could merit in the fullest sense of the word. Merit, it is true, comes from the interior act, but we have seen that Christ's Passion was entirely voluntary in spite of the external violence of his enemies. The merits of Christ on the Cross are to be added to the merits of his life from the very beginning, and their effect is different from all his other merits: the effect is redemption, which the other and preceding merits of Christ did not possess. Says St. Thomas:

> The Passion had a certain effect which his previous merits did not have; not because there was a greater charity, but on account of the special nature of the work which was appropriate to such an effect (III, q. 48, a. 1, ad 3).

The satisfaction of Christ on the Cross was not only sufficient but superabundant in order to atone for all the sins in the world. The measure of this satisfaction may be taken from three considerations. There is first the greatness of his charity, that made him submit to the Passion; secondly there is the dignity of his life, which he laid down as the price of this satisfaction and which being the life of God and man, had infinite value; thirdly there is the extent of the sufferings and pains that he endured. It is to be remembered also that Christ atoned in his death for the crime of those who put him to death; the guilt of the deicides could not in any way diminish the perfection of the satisfaction given Christ. Christ on the Cross was a sacrifice in the fullest sense of the word:

> This voluntary enduring of the Passion was most acceptable to God as coming from charity. Therefore it is manifest that Christ's Passion was a true sacrifice. *Hoc ipsum quod voluntariae passionem sustinuit, Deo maxime acceptum fuit, utpote ex charitate maxima proveniens. Unde manifestum est quod passio Christi fuerit verum sacrificium* (III, q. 48, a. 3).

This sacrifice of Christ was prefigured by the ancient sacrifices. We must bear in mind, however, that in the multiplicity of the ancient sacrifices none of them was a perfect type of the sacrifice of Christ, which is a sacrifice entirely *sui generis*, "one of a kind." But in their multiplicity the sacrifices contained, now one, now another aspect of the sacrifice of Christ as S. Augustine, quoted by St. Thomas, says:

> The primitive sacrifices of the holy Fathers were many and various signs of this true sacrifice, one being prefigured by many, in the same way as a single concept of thought is expressed in many words, in order to commend it without tediousness. *Hujus veri sacrificii multiplicia variaque signa erant sacrificia prisca Sanctorum, cum hoc unum per multa figuraretur, tanquam verbis multis res una diceretur, ut sine fastidio multum commendaretur* (III, q. 48, a. 3).

The words of St. Thomas in his answer are also precious:

> Christ's Passion was indeed a crime on his slayers' part; but on his own it was the sacrifice of one suffering out of charity. *Passio Christi ex parte occidentium ipsum fuit maleficium: sed ex parte ipsius ex charitate patientis fuit sacrificium* (III, q. 48, a. 3, ad 3).

Redemption or the setting free of man is the most constant attribute predicated of Christ's Passion. The captivity from which man is redeemed is the captivity of Satan. Redemption does not, of course, mean that the price is to be paid to Satan but to God, as God through a just judgment had delivered man unto Satan in punishment for sin. St. Thomas concludes:

> And therefore justice required man's redemption with regard to God, but not with regard to the devil. *Et ideo per respectum ad Deum justitia exigebat quod homo redimeretur, non autem per respectum ad diabolum* (III, q. 48, a. 4, ad 1).

The death of Christ may be taken in a twofold sense: *in fieri et in facto esse*, "In the thing being done and in the same thing having been done, [that is, in the actions resulting in Christ's death (*in fieri*) and in the death itself (*in facto esse*)]. In the first acceptation, by "death of Christ" we really mean the whole mystery of his Passion which from its very nature had resulted in death, otherwise it would not have been a supreme act of love. In this sense the death of Christ is the same mystery as his sacrifice. Death, *in facto esse*, means that state of separation between soul and body which was Christ's condition until the Resurrection after he had expired on the Cross. It might be said that death *in fieri* is the pouring out of his blood and therefore a sacrifice. Death *in facto esse* is the separation between soul and body. In this latter sense the death of Christ has redeeming power, not through merit but through efficacy, as have all the states of Christ: because, as St. Thomas says repeatedly, Christ's humanity being the instrument of his divinity brings about *per modum efficientiae*, "by way of efficiency," a corresponding result. Thus *per modum efficientiae* the Resurrection, in its time, effects man's bodily resurrection, and Christ's death causes the death of sin according to the well-known language of St. Paul.

Considering, then, death *in facto esse*, in the state of separation between soul and body, the question asked is this: was divinity separated from the body in Christ's death? The answer is, of course, in the negative. Christ's body was united to divinity hypostatically, therefore physical death could by no means affect this union, any more than death can separate the soul of man from grace.

The same answer is to be given, for the same reasons, to the question whether Christ's divinity in death was separated from the soul. Soul and body were separated but they remained united in one hypostasis, the hypostasis of the Word, just as before death; the hypostatic union was in no way modified through the natural separation between soul and body. The one hypostasis of the Word was at the same [time] hypostasis of the Word, of the soul and of the body. It is therefore to be admitted that in death the personality of Christ was not broken up, but only his human nature was broken up. So we speak of the dead Christ as we speak of the living Christ, as of a complete personality. In very truth the Son of God died, was buried, went down to hell. There is no alteration in the subject of all such phrases.

It would be wrong, however, to say that Christ remained man in death; by man we mean the complete being composed of soul and body. Christ was a spirit in his soul, Christ was a corpse in his body, but though he was a complete Person he was not man.

In this matter of Christ's death the whole theology of hypostatic union is seen in its full import. So, very consistently, St. Thomas affirms that the whole Christ was in the sepulcher and at the same time the whole Christ was in hell:

We have to say, therefore, that during the three days of Christ's death the whole Christ (*totus Christus*) was in the sepulcher because the whole Person was there through the body united with it (the Person) and the whole Christ was in hell because the Person of Christ was there on account of the soul united with it. Moreover, the whole Christ was then everywhere on account of the divine nature. *Totus etiam Christus tunc erat ubique ratione divinae naturae* (III, q. 52, a. 3).

Though Christ in his death is said to have taken upon himself the death of man we are not on this account to forget that he did so with the view of healing the wound of death in human nature. Accordingly Christ in his death did not adopt such features of death as were not conducive to the end of the spiritual raising up of man, nor was there in the dead Christ any kind of corruption or decomposition of the elements of the body. Herein the death of Christ differs profoundly from the ordinary death of man; but in this there is no loss to man's salvation, but a great gain:

> If, however, his body had decayed, or corrupted, this would have been greatly to the detriment of human salvation, for it could not be believed that divine power was in him. *Si autem corpus ejus fuisset putrefactum, vel resolutum, magis hoc fuisset in detrimentum salutis humanae, dum non crederetur in eo esse virtus divina* (III, q. 51, a. 3, ad 1).

17

THE RESURRECTION AND ASCENSION OF CHRIST

CHRIST'S RESURRECTION MEANS MORE THAN THE vivifying of a dead body; it means above all things that mode of existence which is called the life of glory. It is in this sense chiefly that the Resurrection has become the central mystery of Christianity. If by resurrection we meant nothing more than the fact that the Christ killed by the Jews was found to be alive again, we should not speak of anything more marvellous than, say, the resurrection of Lazarus. But resurrection in the Christian sense is something infinitely beyond the raising again of one that was dead: it is a newness of life that transforms the whole history of mankind. With St. Paul and the other Apostles, the great Doctors of the Church have spoken of Christ's Resurrection chiefly from this aspect:

> Christ's soul was glorified from the instant of his conception by a perfect fruition of the Godhead. But it was owing to the divine economy that the glory did not pass from his soul to his body, in order that by the Passion he might accomplish

the mystery of our redemption. Consequently, when the mystery of Christ's Passion and death was finished, straightway the soul communicated its glory to the risen body in the Resurrection; and so that body was made glorious (III, q. 54, a. 3).

Through his Resurrection Christ showed forth the glory that was in him from the beginning. It was not a new glory, but one that had been hidden through charity, through Christ's love for mankind. Even when it is said that Christ merited his exaltation the term "merit" is used very relatively; it implies that, having done his task of redemption through the humility of the Cross, all the special *dispensatio*, "dispensation," that kept his glory from the eyes of men and from portions of his own human nature had come to an end and the Son of God appeared in his native glory. The Church's rejoicing at Easter is the joy of one who has found her bridegroom set free from all the trammels of death with which he had bound himself.

An easily understood gradation may be cited here. There is first the miracle of a dead person being given life again; then there is secondly the additional divine favor that this person thus restored to life be given a state of glory which he did not possess before in any sense, though he may have merited it through deeds of sanctity; and thirdly there is this restoration of a person to his native estate, an estate momentarily forgone from charity. This last is the real and the full meaning of Christ's Resurrection and it is herein that the Resurrection has its full power as a testimony. This third sense implies, of course, the two preceding ones, but in it alone we have the full significance of Christ's words: "Ought not Christ to have suffered these things and so to enter into his glory" (Luke 24:26)?

As a consequence of this innate though hidden power of Christ it may be said that Christ rose from the dead in virtue of his own superiority over death. The true Christian phrase is that Christ rose from the dead, though of course we also find the other expression that God raised up Christ from the grave. It is worth our while to quote St. Thomas fully, as he gives us a further brilliant exposé of the doctrine of the Hypostatic Union:

> In consequence of death, Christ's Godhead was not separated from his soul, nor from his flesh. Consequently, both the soul and the flesh of the dead Christ can be considered in two respects: first in respect of his Godhead; secondly in respect of his created nature. Therefore, according to the virtue of the Godhead united to it the body took back again the soul which it had laid aside, and the soul took back again the body which it had abandoned: and thus Christ rose by his own power. And this is precisely what is written: "For although he was crucified through (our) weakness, yet he liveth by the power of God" (2 Cor 8:4). But if we consider the body and soul of the dead Christ according to the power of created nature, they could not thus be reunited, but it was necessary for Christ to be raised up by God (III, q. 53, a. 4).

We have here another instance of the *communicatio idiomatum*. The same Person can be said to rise from the dead and to be raised from the dead. He rises in virtue of his divinity, he is raised in his humanity. But the greater truth is this, that he himself broke the fetters of death.

Nothing is more constant in the Apostolic writings than to attribute to Christ's Resurrection far-reaching causality in the work of salvation. St. Paul's text from the Romans may suffice: "Who (Christ) was delivered up for our sins, and rose again for our justification" (Rom 4:25).

We certainly should not do justice to Christ's Resurrection if we saw in it no more than a glorious event that crowned his earthly career without having any soteriological import. Christ's Resurrection, on the contrary, is part of the work of salvation.

I hope I am not hypercritical in blaming the modern tendencies which have so completely and exclusively identified Christ's Passion and death with salvation that there is no room left for the Resurrection as an agent of redemption. The older views of Christ's redemptive work had a broader basis. There are certain effects which do seem to belong exclusively to the Passion and the death, such as merit and sacrifice; but there are other redemptive activities which are to be predicated of the Resurrection in a most excellent fashion. It is not desirable to make precise distinctions as to the effects on man's salvation that proceed, on the one hand from Christ's Passion and death and from his Resurrection on the other hand. Most likely such exact divisions of labor do not exist at all in the divine economy of Christ. Setting apart certain clear factors which are evidently inseparable from the death of the Son of God, it is much more according to the spirit of Christian antiquity to consider our Lord's Resurrection as an endless source of newness of life.

I quote here two passages from the Summa which are precise without becoming exclusive. Their perusal will leave the reader free to attach to Christ's Resurrection immense spiritual efficacy, equally with that element of testimony which nowadays seems to be our only concern when we preach on the Easter mystery:

> Considered on the part of their efficiency, which is dependent on the divine power, both Christ's death and his Resurrection are the cause both of the destruction of death and of the renewal of life: but con-

sidered as exemplar causes, Christ's death—by which he withdrew from mortal life—is the cause of the destruction of our death; while his Resurrection, whereby he inaugurated immortal life, is the cause of the repairing of our life. But Christ's Passion is furthermore a meritorious cause, as stated above (III, q. 56, a. 1, ad 4).

Two things concur in the justification of souls, namely, forgiveness of sin and newness of life through grace. Consequently, as to efficacy, which comes of the Divine power, the Passion as well as the Resurrection of Christ is the cause of justification as to both the above. But as to exemplarity, properly speaking, Christ's Passion and death is the cause of the forgiveness of guilt, by which forgiveness we die unto sin: whereas Christ's Resurrection is the cause of newness of life, which comes through grace or justice: consequently the Apostle says *that he was delivered up*, i.e. to death—*for our sins*—i.e. to take them away—*and rose again for our justification* (Rom 4:25). But Christ's Passion was also a meritorious cause, as stated above (III, q. 56, a. 2, ad 4).

Ascension into heaven has never, in Christian liturgy, been given the importance which attaches to Christ's Resurrection from the dead. This has sometimes surprised the simple-minded. Going up to heaven appears to be so great an achievement that even rising from the dead may pale before it. In this we find our Christology at its best. The one supreme fact in Christ's career is that he should be in the fullness of his Godhead, no longer in the "state of a slave," *forma servi*. This was accomplished in the Resurrection; in fact, this is Resurrection. Ascending to heaven is an external accident, however glorious and spectacular it may be.

To the Ascension as well as to the Resurrection, soteriological significance is to be attached. It is truly the cause of our own future exaltation, not meritoriously, but as exemplar and as the efficient cause, just as the Resurrection is the exemplar and the efficient cause of our future bodily resurrection.

There is, however, another soteriological element mentioned in connection with Christ's Ascension into heaven to which St. Paul has given great relief:

> For Jesus is not entered into the Holies made with hands, the patterns of the true: but into Heaven itself, that he may appear now in the presence of God for us (Heb 9:24).

This appearing in the presence of God for us may be interpreted either as an active intercession or as a presentation of his merits as the permanent price of our redemption.

18

The Exaltation of Christ

THE OLDEST FORMULA FOR EXPRESSING THE EXALTATION of the Word Incarnate is well known to all Christians. Christ is said to sit at the right hand of God, at the right hand of the Father. The grand metaphor occurs a dozen times in the New Testament writings, not including the allusions to and the paraphrases of the 109th Psalm: *Dixit Dominus Domino meo, sede a dextris meis.* [The Lord said to my Lord, sit at my right hand] (Ps 109:1). Perhaps the most powerful rendering of this truly apostolic notion is found in St. Peter's first Epistle:

> Jesus Christ, who is on the right hand of God, swallowing down death that we might be made heirs of life everlasting: being gone into heaven, the angels and powers and virtues being made subject to him (1 Pet 3:22).

The earliest form, however, and one that is descriptive of something actually seen, is to be found in the Acts, in connection with the death of Stephen the deacon:

But he, being full of the Holy Ghost, looking up steadfastly to heaven, saw the glory of God and Jesus standing on the right hand of God (Acts 7:55).

The completeness of Christ's triumph was, indeed, an idea very dear to the Apostolic age, and those who had seen the humiliation of Jesus, as had the Apostles themselves, never wearied of the contrast between the abasement of his death and the "glories that should follow," *et posteriores glorias* (1 Pet. 1:11).

It is evident that at no time could it enter the minds of those early Christians that Christ's existence in heaven could be anything but supremest bliss and glory. Christian worship of those ages is the worship of an omnipotent and triumphant Savior. It is, perhaps, easier to see the appropriateness of the ancient metaphor than to analyze it or give it exact meaning; we may, however, take as a full rendering of it the saying of St. Thomas that the *sessio ad dexteram Patris*, "the sitting at the right hand of the Father," means three realities, namely, the glory of the Divinity, eternal blessedness, and God's power as Judge. Christ has entered into participation of those divine privileges:

> To sit on the right hand of the Father is nothing else than to share in the glory of the Godhead with the Father, and to possess beatitude and judiciary power, and that unchangeable and regally. *Unde sedere ad dexteram Patris nihil aliud est quam simul cum Patre habere gloriam divinitatis, et beatitudinem et judiciariam potestatem, et hoc immutabiliter et regaliter* (III, q. 58, a. 2).

It is true, indeed, that the human nature of the glorified Christ is always infinitely inferior to Deity itself; but the Person, Christ, composed of divinity and humanity, is infinitely above all that could be called suffering. During his mortal life it could be said with all exactness of language that he suffered. Not so now. In fact the immunity of the Person is the immunity of the human nature also. There is now none of that special dispensation which made it possible for Christ to suffer in soul and body during the days of his earthly career. The contrast between our Lord's condition of life now and that which he accepted in his mortal frame is one of the great sources of inspiration for the sacred writers. We all love the sound of St. Paul's great text on that very subject, one of the commonplaces of ecclesiastical music as well as of theology:

> He humbled himself becoming obedient unto death, even to the death of the cross. For which cause, God also hath exalted him and hath given him a name which is above all names: that in the name of Jesus every knee should bow, of those that are in heaven, on earth, and under the earth (Phil 2:8-10).

It is, of course, self-evident that the Christ to whom the Apostles prayed was the Lord of Glory, and as Lord of Glory they loved him and held mystical intercourse with him. The rapture of St. John when he was in the Spirit on the Lord's day brought him to the feet of "One like the Son of Man" (Rev 1:13) whose majesty so overpowered the disciple that he "fell to the ground as one dead" (Rev 1:17).

It is difficult to reconcile with this traditional Christian faith in Christ's exaltation some recent expressions of devotional sentiment or even certain theological opinions. There is no other inferiority in Christ than the fact that his human nature is a created, finite nature. There could not be predicated of Christ, in his present heavenly state, the attitude of victim before God. To regard him now as a *sacrificium coeleste*, a "heavenly sacrifice," would imply contradiction as it would include in the same Person, Christ, final exaltation and permanent inferiority.

Now it is true that we have the solemn assurance that Christ is a priest forever; he is a priest in heaven, in his glorious state; but this does not mean that he is a victim for ever. St. Thomas has written one of his most satisfying articles on this subject:

> In the priestly office, we may consider two things: first, the offering of the sacrifice; secondly, the consummation of the sacrifice, consisting in this, that those for whom the sacrifice is offered, obtain the end of the sacrifice. Now, the end of the sacrifice which Christ offered consisted not in temporal but in eternal good, which we obtain through his death, according to Hebrews 9:11: *Christ is a high-priest of the good things to come*; for which reason the priesthood of Christ is said to be eternal. Now, this consummation of Christ's sacrifice was foreshadowed in this, that the high-priest of the Old Law, once a year, entered into the Holy of holies with the blood of a he-goat and a calf, as laid down (Lev 16:11); and yet he offered up the he-goat and the calf not within the Holy of holies, but without. In like manner Christ entered into the Holy of holies—that is, into heaven—and prepared the way for us, that we might enter by the virtue of his blood, which he shed for us on earth (III, q. 22, a. 5).

Much confusion of thought could be avoided if these doctrines concerning the true nature of Christ's priestly office in heaven were more generally accepted and assimilated. We should not then be obliged to reconcile the irreconcilable, the state of glory and the state of victim, which it is the fashion of some theologians to confound. The Eucharistic sacrifice on the Christian altars on this earth in no wise alters the fullness of glory, as this sacrifice is not in Christ's natural state, but in his sacramental state.

No suffering, no humiliation, no inferiority of any kind can be predicated with any truthfulness of Christ since the day of his exaltation. It would be a denial of that very elevation itself, which is the sure basis of orthodox Christology. We are aware of the fact that much in modern devotional phraseology sounds as if Christ were not in perfect exaltation, as if he were oppressed with sadness by the injustices of his people. The Person of Christ has been, and is, the center of a whole literature of sympathy and condolence, such as has not been bestowed on anyone else.

This, of course, has an explanation that saves its orthodoxy. There is first that vivid remembrance of Christ's sufferings and the indignities he bore when he was on this earth. It is a supreme sign of love to keep fresh that memory, to dwell on the death of the Lord as if one were contemplating it with one's eyes. The words of the prophet Zacharias are aptly quoted in this connection:

> And I will pour out upon the house of David and upon the inhabitants of Jerusalem the spirit of grace and of prayers: and they shall look upon me, whom they have pierced. And they shall mourn for him as one mourneth for an only son: and they shall grieve over him, as the manner is to grieve for the death of the first-born (Zech 12:10).

Then there is the great mystical meaning of Christ suffering in his members. There seems to be endless scope for the mystic to weep over his Lord, ill-treated and trodden under foot in this vicarious fashion in the Church that is his body. We must, however, confess to the impression that careful examination of a good deal of the more

recent devotional literature has left in our mind, that much impru-
dent language is current, and for many souls, well-meaning indeed
but ill-instructed, the Person of Christ is beheld as an actual sufferer.
Such an attitude, indulged in habitually, for it really is sentimental
indulgence, would be found to falsify the position of the redeemed
soul towards its Redeemer. If there is peril the danger signal will be
given in due time by the watchman in Peter's boat.

The state of exaltation in Christ has to be considered as an immense, an infinite activity. Christ is the Judge of the living and the
dead. He carries out the great judgements of God's justice now, in
this present time, even before the final and universal Judgement at
the end of the world. It is an integral portion of our faith in the Incarnate Son of God to regard him as the arbiter of human destinies.
Christians ought to have no sentimental difficulties in this matter
of Christ's juridical role. Love, even tenderness of love, ought to go
hand in hand with immeasurable awe at the thought of the greatness
of the judgements delivered by the Holy One. Our Christ is truly a
militant God. He is the Lord of innumerable spiritual battles, One
that is born for the wards of giants:

> And I saw heaven opened: and behold a white horse. And he
> that sat upon him was called faithful and true: and with justice
> doth he judge and fight (Rev 19:11).